Routledge Revivals

History of the First Twelve Years of the Reign of Mai Idris Alooma of Bornu (1571 - 1583)

History of the First Twelve Years of the Reign of Mai Idris Alooma of Bornu (1571 - 1583)

By his Imam,
Ahmed Ibn Fartua

Together with the
"Diwan of the Sultans of Bornu"

and
" Girgam" of the Magumi

Translated from the Arabic with an Introduction and Notes
by
H. R. PALMER

First published in 1926 by Frank Cass and Company Limited
by arrangement with the Federal Government o f Nigeria

This edition first published in 2018 by Routledge
2 Park Square, Milton Park, Abingdon, Oxon, OX14 4RN
and by Routledge
52 Vanderbilt Avenue, New York, NY 10017, USA

Routledge is an imprint of the Taylor & Francis Group, an informa business

© 1926 by Taylor and Francis

All rights reserved. No part of this book may be reprinted or reproduced or utilised in any form or by any electronic, mechanical, or other means, now known or hereafter invented, including photocopying and recording, or in any information storage or retrieval system, without permission in writing from the publishers.

Publisher's Note
The publisher has gone to great lengths to ensure the quality of this reprint but points out that some imperfections in the original copies may be apparent.

Disclaimer
The publisher has made every effort to trace copyright holders and welcomes correspondence from those they have been unable to contact.

A Library of Congress record exists under ISBN: 78066844

ISBN 13: 978-0-367-13490-7 (hbk)
ISBN 13: 978-0-367-13491-4 (pbk)
ISBN 13: 978-0-429-02678-2 (ebk)

CASS LIBRARY OF AFRICAN STUDIES

GENERAL STUDIES

No. 92

Editorial Adviser: JOHN RALPH WILLIS
Department of History, University of California, Berkeley

History of the
First Twelve Years of the Reign of
Mai Idris Alooma of Bornu
(1571–1583)

History of the First Twelve Years of the Reign of Mai Idris Alooma of Bornu (1571–1583)

By his Imam,
Ahmed Ibn Fartua

Together with the
"Diwan of the Sultans of Bornu"
and
"Girgam" of the Magumi

Translated from the Arabic with an Introduction and Notes
by
H. R. PALMER

FRANK CASS & CO. LTD.
1970

Published by
FRANK CASS AND COMPANY LIMITED
67 Great Russell Street, London WC1B 3BT
by arrangement with the Federal Government of Nigeria

All rights reserved

| First edition | 1926 |
| New impression | 1970 |

ISBN 0 7146 1709 1

Printed in Great Britain by Clarke, Doble & Brendon Ltd.
Plymouth and London

History of the First Twelve Years of the Reign of Mai Idris Alooma of Bornu (1571—1583)

By his Imam, Ahmed ibn Fartua

Together with the
"Diwan of the Sultans of Bornu"
and
"Girgam" of the Magumi

Translated from the Arabic with Introduction and Notes by H. R. Palmer, sometime Resident of Bornu Province.

PRINTED BY THE GOVERNMENT PRINTER, LAGOS.

1926.

PREFACE.

THE extensive Province of Bornu situated in the North-eastern corner of Nigeria and bounded on the East by the shores of Lake Chad has a peculiar fascination both for the traveller and for the ethnologist.

In the southern portions of the Province which attain a level of about 2,000 feet above the sea both climate and scenery are delightful while the presence in many parts of elephant, antelope, gazelle and an immense variety of bird life is a source of constant attraction to the sportsman.

The Kanuri, a people of Barbar extraction, are the most important tribe in the kingdom of Bornu, next in importance come the Arabs (known locally as Shuwa), the Fulani (Fellata) and a considerable number of still primitive pagans. The ruling classes are Muhammadan and although the Province contains several independent Emirs, they all look up to the Shehu of Bornu as their spiritual head. The population of Bornu exceeds a million and although of very mixed and sometimes uncertain origin the races comprised therein are all of them strikingly virile.

In the political development of the Western Sudan the kingdom of Bornu has played a notable part. At one time or another the influence of its rulers extended far beyond the limits of the present Nigerian Province. What is still more significant is the fact that it possesses a recorded history reading back as far as the tenth century A.D. The elucidation of this history and the investigation of the traditions and customs of the Bornu people have received a marked impetus in recent years from the studies of Mr. H. R. Palmer, formerly the Resident of the Bornu Province and now the Lieutenant-Governor of the Northern Provinces, who now by his excellent translation entitled " A history of the first twelve years of the reign of Mai Idris Alooma " and by the most interesting historical and ethnological notes which he has supplied to illuminate the text has shed a new light on the life, civilisation and mode of thought of an African Muhammadan king during the 16th century.

The narrative of Ahmed ibn Fartua is not only picturesque in form, but if due allowance is made for the customary adulation of a reigning prince by his humble servitor decidedly bears the imprint of truth.

That Mai Idris was the great warrior he is described to be may be open to doubt. The employment of Turkish musketeers against an enemy armed with bows, arrows and spears would appear to have loaded the dice in his favour. Nor is it possible to believe that his series of victorious campaigns during a period of twelve years could have been conducted with the loss of only three men as recorded by his chronicler, " the Muslims all returning in the belly of the night safe and with booty."

Nevertheless there is no doubt that Sultan Idris in the conduct of these campaigns showed considerable strategical skill, made the most of his advantage in armament and extended his sphere of influence as far as the Sahara in the North, almost to the gates of Kano in the West, to the Cameroons in the East and to the region of the present Emirate of Biu in the South.

Moreover, there is evidence in the narrative that Mai Idris was an enlightened ruler and a sound administrator. He sought not to interfere with the administration of justice, leaving that to the judges. He introduced a strict code of morals to the intense surprise of his chronicler and encouraged the peaceful arts of agriculture, architecture and boat construction.

The narrative while of undoubted historical value is also very quaint and attractive to the reader and Mr. Palmer is to be congratulated on having added a material contribution to the history of a Province with which his name will always be associated.

GRAEME THOMSON.

Government House,
    Lagos,
        6th December, 1926.

INTRODUCTION.

The Arabic manuscript of the document which is here translated, was obtained by the traveller Dr. Heinrich Barth at Kukawa, the capital of the Kanembu Shehus of Bornu, about the year 1853 from the then Wazir of Bornu, Haj Beshir. It was sent by Dr. Barth to the British Foreign Office from whence in some mysterious way it wandered to Germany, where at the instance of the Secretary of State for the Colonies it was found, and photographed by the courtesy of the German authorities in the year 1921.

The manuscript was called by Dr. Barth "A history of the first twelve years of the reign of Mai (king) Idris Alooma." That is therefore probably the most suitable title for it. It embraces accounts of the various expeditions or wars undertaken by that monarch between the year 1571 when he ascended the throne, and about the year 1583, excluding his expeditions to Kanem, East of Lake Chad which were treated of in a subsequent work. It was thus written in the year A.H. 990 or 991, *i.e.*, 1582/83 A.D.

The compilation is of considerable interest from many points of view, but it is especially valuable as a picture of the life, and mode of thought of an African Muslim, Amir ul Muminin, or Caliph, during the 16th century of our era, as well as being a very accurate basis from which to judge of the history and development of the peoples of the regions to which it relates since the day of Idris Alooma, that is to say, during the last 400 years.

The kingdom or empire—as it subsequently became—of Bornu had its beginnings somewhere in the regions which are now called Borku and Wadai, probably within 200 years of the opening of the Muhammadan era. The first rulers were clearly chiefs who lived in tents and ruled over nomads. Their ancestor, whoever he was, had married a woman of the Barbar tribe of Kayi—a branch of the peoples now called Zaghawa and Beli. (Bideyat.)

According to the preponderance of Bornu tradition which, it must be noted, is Muslim tradition, the epoch at which this rule or kingdom arose was contemporary with the time of the death of the Ummeyad Caliph Umr ibn Abd ul Aziz, for it is said that after the time of this Caliph, the Caliphate passed to Bornu. We may therefore date the rise of the Bornu Kingdom in the Wadai region as between 750 and 800 A.D. and it seems probable that this ignoring of the Abbasid Caliphate by the Bornu historians or traditionalists, means that Islam was introduced into Wadai and Kanem by adherents of the Fatimid (Shi'ite) dynasty of Egypt, which (founded at Mahdiyyah in Tunis in 909 A.D.) became established in Cairo in 969, where its princes reigned, till ousted from power by one of their own generals, Saladin, who founded the Ayyubid dynasty in Egypt in 1174 A.D.

The age of Saladin is almost contemporaneous with that of the second Muslim Mai of Kanem—Mai Dunama—who was drowned while on a pilgrimage to Mecca near Suez possibly at the port of Berinice (Barnik)—circa 1150 A.D.

During these centuries the Christian West had remained ignorant, rude, and barbarous, while Saracenic culture passed on the torch of civilisation to future ages. The nascent kingdom of Bornu drew its inspiration from Egypt and North Africa. Though its conduct towards the African peoples by which it was surrounded was callous and brutal, the degree of civilisation achieved by its early chiefs would appear to compare favourably with that of European monarchs of that day. It was probably during the 12th century that a settled capital was founded at N'jimi (Sima) near Mao, in Kanem, East of Lake Chad. From thence a redoubtable warrior, Mai Dunama Dabalemi, early in the 13th century extended the Bornu empire up to Kauwar and Tibesti in the North, and to the regions South-west of Lake Chad.

The early or " golden age " of Islam, received its first great check in 1213 A.D. when Spanish Islam was broken at the great battle of Las Navas de Tolosa by the Christian forces of Castile. It would appear that before that time North African influences, Almoravid or Almohad, as appears from documents found at Tuwat, were powerful in Bornu. The Hafside dynasty of Tunis had also lent a helping hand to its Sudanese contemporary. (Ibn Khaldun.)

The successors of Saladin, within fifty years of the date of his death, had all power taken from them in Egypt by their Turkish slaves the Mamluks, who later, in the time of Beybars (1260-1277) sought a sanction for the continued enjoyment of power by inviting an uncle of the last Abbasid Caliph, who had managed to escape the Bagdad massacre of 1258, to come to Cairo as Caliph in 1261.

It was about the time of the fall of Bagdad also that Abu Abdullah Muhammad (1249-1277) of the Hafside dynasty in Tunis called himself " Khalifa " and " Amir ul Muminin."

His father Yahya though virtually independent had been the Tunisian Governor of the Almohad dynasty of Morocco. Abu Abdullah is said to have been prompted to take the title of " Caliph " by the Sharif of Mecca.

It was thus at the close of the period rendered illustrious for Bornu by Dunama Dabalemi (1221-1259), that there occurred the event which changed the face of Islam, and affected the history of the civilised world to an extent which it is difficult to estimate, namely the sack of Bagdad by the Mongols under Hulagu Khan. It hardly needs demonstration that this event must have caused an increased number of itinerant Arab divines to go West, and enter Egypt and Africa, taking with them the teaching of the various Tarikas of Islam which had arisen in Irak.

In the succeeding century there ensued in Bornu a civil war between the legitimate Kanem dynasty and their cousins on the mother's side, the tribe of Kayi or Bulala, who had established themselves in the region of Lake Fittri, the Kanem Mai (Mai Daud Nigaleme) being expelled from his capital N'jimi about 1386 A.D., and his house finally evacuating Kanem about 1400 A.D.

The time of Daud's expulsion and beginning of the civil war in Kanem thus synchronised with the reign of the Turkish Sultan

Introduction. 3

Bayazid I who was finally defeated and taken prisoner by Timur in 1402.

Constantinople was taken by Muhammad II in 1453. Muhammad II was succeeded by Bayazid II (1481-1512), and the latter by Salim I (1512-1521), in whose time the puppet Abbasid Caliph in Egypt, Mutawakkil, is said, probably quite falsely, to have ceded the office of Khalifa to the Turks.

In any case Salim I had the Khutbah read in his own name at Cairo on 23rd January, 1517, and was then saluted as " The victorious king, Sultan Salim Shah." * It is an echo of this address which we probably find in this history, in the use of the title ' Shah ' for the Mai of Bornu.

Again, the fame of the Saljuks of " Rum " and an extant letter from Timur written to Bayazid II in 1401 A.D. in which he begins " O king in Rum Yilderim Bayazid " seem to suggest that the " mosque of the Armi ", spoken of by Imam Ahmad in " The Kanem War," was possibly a mosque founded by Turks, called Rumi, from the name of the kingdom they had conquered and displaced though it is perhaps more probable that Armi has its usual Sudanese meaning of Moroccan or North African " sharp-shooter," and denotes Islamic Barbars from the North or North-West who came to Bornu.

The civil war which supervened after the death of Dunama Dabalemi dislocated the contact of Bornu with the outside world from the middle of the 14th century to the end of the 15th century, when the dynasty established itself West of Lake Chad at N'gazargamu under Mai 'Ali Ghaji Dunamami, and revived its power and prestige.

The Osmanli Turks having extinguished the Roman Byzantine Empire by taking Constantinople in 1453, had within a century thereafter conquered the Islamic East from Persia to Morocco, subjugated the whole Balkan peninsular, and advanced through Hungary to the walls of Vienna.

About the year 1507, Idris Katagarmabe, the son of 'Ali Ghaji Dunamami, founder of N'gazargamu, and grandfather of Idris Alooma, with the record of whose reign this history deals, had been able in some measure to re-establish the authority of the royal house over Kanem and the Bulala who had ruled Kanem from Fittri since about 1400 A.D.

The warlike exploits of this Mai Idris Katagarmabe were recorded by his chief Imam, Sheikh Masfarma or Masbarma, in a work still known as the Tarikh Masbarma, a work on which the writer of this history, the Imam ibn Fartua, obviously drew for information concerning events which took place prior to the time which was within the memory of himself or people still alive in his day.

That a copy or copies of this Tarikh Masbarma still exist seems probable, for I have been promised copies more than once, but for some reason or other they are jealously guarded by those who possess them, probably in a large measure because it is thought

---

* For this and other information I am indebted to " The Caliphate " by Sir T. W. Arnold, C.I.E., Litt. D., Oxford, 1924.

that their production would be distasteful to the present ruling dynasty of Kanembu.

It is very evident, however, from fragmentary and often mutilated documents relating to the times of the earlier Mais or Sultans of Kanem, which are still extant, that though the royal line (the Magumi) was continuous from the beginning (750 to 800 A.D.) till it was superseded by the Kanembu Kuburi about 1810, yet there were fundamental differences between the Bornu (Kanem) Kingdom as it existed at the time of the death of Dunama Dabalemi about 1259 A.D. and the revived Bornu Kingdom which was established by 'Ali Ghaji Dunamami at N'gazargamu about 1470 A.D. after the civil war with the Bulala.

The earlier kingdom was a rule established by camel-men—Barbar tribes akin to the modern Tuwareg races, called in the Sudan Zaghawa, Amakitan or Keyi (Kayi)—over the negro (So) tribes extending from Lake Chad East to Borku and Wadai. These monarchs conquered the Teda or Tebu races (Garamantes) which lay to the North of them, though they solidified their position in that region by marrying into the Tebu royal clan of Tumagari.

Though, however, they adopted a language of Kanem (now Kanuri) akin to the Tebu tongue, they remained a Barbar territorial aristocracy cognate to the other Barbars, the Sanhaja, Zaghawa, Lamta, Lamtuna, etc., who roamed over the Sahara.

It is uncertain at what date their kinsmen further East—other clans of the Kayi (Zaghawa)—came down to the region of Lake Fittri from Wadai, but evidently that took place some time after 1259 A.D.* It was the fusion of these new clans of Kayi with the inhabitants of the Fittri region (called in the traditions N'gizim) which gave rise to the separate political entity which arose in this Fittri region about 1350 A.D. and was called Bulala—the " kingdom of Gaoga " of Leo Africanus.

It is extremely probable that the Bulala owed their initial successes over the legitimate royal dynasty to Tebu intrigue and help, but—at any rate, in the later stages of the conflict—it became a regular practice for scions of the royal house who were in difficulties to become absorbed in Tebu clans together with their followers.

As the Tebu elements would seem even then to have outnumbered the Barbar elements in Kanem and Bornu, and, as we know that there was in being a general westward drift of the Tuwareg races towards the Atlantic, it is hardly surprising that when the civil war ended, the Barbar or Zaghawa Kingdom of Bornu became to all intents and purposes a Tebu Kingdom, or at least a kingdom in which the aristocracy were predominantly of Teda or Tebu connection though still called—as they are to this day called by their western neighbours—Beriberi (Barbars).

It appears doubtful from the records and traditions whether the Bulala of Fittri ever really administered Kanem. The old capital N'jimi was apparently deserted from the time Mai Umr

---

* In the " Kanem War " it is stated that there were no Bulala in the days of Dunama Dabalemi.

had to leave it in 1389. It is probable that the reason the Bornu Mais did not go back to it, after the time when they ceased to fear the Bulala about 1507, was the preponderance in Kanem by that time of purely Teda tribes, called Gura'an, who were not particularly amenable to settled rule.

It was doubtless both easier and more profitable to wage ' holy war ' as narrated in the work before us, upon the pagan tribes West of Lake Chad than to govern Kanem, while at the same time N'gazargamu was more suitable as a centre from which to control Damagram, and the profitable natron trade of the Kauwar region, and keep touch with Fezzan, then the most important market for the slave trade, than the old capital N'jimi to the East of Lake Chad.

Moreover athwart the direct road to the East from Kanem now lay the Fung dynasty of Senaar on the Blue Nile, and the Christian Dongola Kingdom.

At least one tradition survives of a time when the Meks of Senaar—whether a remnant of the Meroitic Kingdom or not—were in some sense either theoretically subject to or at least connected with the early Bornu Mais of Wadai, and there is good reason for thinking that the Kayi or Keyi were at one time, probably before 750 A.D. located in the region of the Wadi Malik, West of Dongola.

All that had, however, by 1470 passed away, and the main routes of Ali Ghaji Dunamami and his descendants to the East lay through Tragen or Zeila in Fezzan or Kufra, and Masr (Cairo).

It is apparent from various notices in Arab authors, particularly Yakubi, that a large number of merchants and others from Khorasan and other parts of Asia had settled in Fezzan as early as 900 A.D. to engage in the slave trade, and it is doubtless from those sources that certain traces of Persian or Shi'ite influence which are observable in the narrative, came—as for instance the use of the word ' musjid ' in one passage, for mosque.

In fact it is extremely probable that the famous Sheikh Masbarma, who migrated to Bornu from Fezzan, was one of these people from Iran or Irak and that he introduced Eastern or Asiatic ideas, for there exists even now a strange religious community in the region in which Sheikh Masbarma and his descendants settled (near Gumsa), which, though tolerated, is regarded as unorthodox and seems to have some strange esoteric rites reminiscent of dervish fraternities in the East.

It is observable also that within 100 years of the date of the conquest of Constantinople by the Turks, Idris Alooma, as we see in this narrative, had as mercenaries Turkish musketeers. The keeping open of all routes from the Mediterranean and Egypt was at least one of the objects of the expedition to the Kauwar oasis which is narrated in these pages. Doubtless during the civil war the control of that oasis, formerly subject to the Mais of N'jimi, had reverted to the Tebu.

The Asben oasis on the other hand, originally peopled by negroes comparable to the earliest Hausa stock of the country to the immediate South, had been conquered before 1150 A.D. by

Barbar tribes of the Zaghawa stock—*i.e.*, Amakitan or tribes cognate to them and the early rulers of Kanem.

These tribes, however, were replaced in the Asben region by northern Tuwareg about 1400 A.D. and the town of Agades was founded. It was thus against these newer tribes of Tuwareg (also called Barbar) that Idris launched the expedition described in this work.

When we come to the country with which most of the narrative is concerned, now British Bornu, it is evident that the Bornu—more correctly Bar-anu (*i.e.*, place of the Bar-an, or Barbars)—of 1570 A.D. was of very small extent, hardly larger than the present district of Geidam in the Bornu Emirate.

The surrounding peoples West and South-west were all pagan negroes of different kinds till one reached in the West the stockade of Dala (*i.e.*, the modern town of Kano), and the land of Fali (*i.e.*, Bauchi and Gombe) at that time dominated by the Kwararafa, and to the South-west the Sultan of Yamta (*i.e.*, the modern Biu Emirate), and the Sultan of Mandara of which Kerawa, just North of the most northerly spurs of the Mandara hills, was the capital.

Not far North of Kerawa lies the site of the famous town of Amsaka, the siege of which is so graphically described. From thence in the country northwards back to Birni (capital of Bornu) on the Komadugu Yobe, dwelt various indigenous peoples cognate to the modern Kotoko and Buduma who in general were called "So."

The central part of British Bornu was occupied by various peoples cognate to the modern N'gizim and Kerri-Kerri of Western Bornu.

We know from other sources and records that at this time Islam had already secured a foothold in Kano, introduced both from North Africa (Sheikh Maghili of Tuwat) and from the Wangara country (Songhay), and that the kings (Sarkis) of the seven Hausa States, Gobir, Katsina, Kano, Buram-ta-Gabbas (near Hadeijia) Rano and Zugzug (Zaria) owed their origin to a Barbar invasion in about 1000 A.D. which was probably a reflex of the tribal movements which had first carried the Kayi Zaghawa into Kanem.

On the other hand, the Sultans of Yamta (Biu) and Mandara were both in some sense descended from the same type of peoples as the ruler of Bornu himself, if they did not actually belong to the Magumi clan, the Wandala of Mandara having a tradition that they were at one time, as was the case with other tribes East of Tibesti, Christians, and that there had settled among them a people called Kindin Kel Burum—*i.e.*, Tuwareg living in the Burum.

There were apparently at that time no Arabs or other peoples, in these regions, and it was thus not till after the ruin of Amsaka that the Iesiye Arabs, a Sudanese branch of the great Beni Hilal, emigrated into the Dikwa region in which they are now very numerous.

Both the name and details given about this town of Amsaka are interesting because there seems to be an idea that its name is cognate to the name of the region to the immediate South of it, Musgu, and to Barth's name for a group of languages spoken in that region—the Masa group—to which the modern Burra and Marghi languages belong. The Tuwareg name " Kel Burum " to which we have referred may also be pertinent.

The word Amsaka seems to be similar to place names like Damasek. They are composed of Ama (people) and an enclitic sek or sak which in the Barbar desert languages means " encampment "—*i.e.*, Amsaka is merely a variant of Sagwa one of various appellations of the Zaghawa of the Sahara in the Arab authors. Amsaka was clearly not part of the Mandara Kingdom but had no doubt affinity both with the so-called " So " cities of Dikwa like N'difu and Sangaya, as well as the historic Waraga Dubuwa region and the famous rock of Balda, to the South, through which passed the great migrations from the East known as those of the Kwararafa into the lower Gongola region.

It is a region also famous in the legends of Mai Dugu Bremmi, probably the first Zaghawa chief of Wadai and Kanem, who, so the story goes, was enticed by a female Jinn through these regions till he reached a point on the left bank of the Sanaga River where he died after founding a great city, the site of which is still said by travellers to be revered by the local natives. It was and still is called Yari Arbasan. The inhabitants of the region are said to retain both the title of the Kanuri war chief Kaigama and a memory of their ancient connection with Bornu and Kanem.

If the words Amsaka and Musgu are derivatives as appears to be the case, of the Tuwareg word sek or sak, that is a very fair indication that the Kel Burum of Mandara legend were Zaghawa, a supposition which is rather enhanced by the fact that the Amsaka people used stones and slings as missiles, a method of fighting which, so far as is known, was not practised by any of these peoples except the Zaghawa.

Further, there is another strong tradition that this same country was at a remote period peopled by Dajo races who spread as far South as Mubi. The Dajo are no doubt identical with the Tajowin " idolaters " of Idrisi—who in his day, 1150 A.D. lived in the region of Fittri, and are by him said to have been a branch of the Zaghawa.

Amsaka as we are told in the narrative was founded before Birni N'gazargamu, *i.e.*, before 1470 A.D. We may infer that it was founded before the era of Bulala and Tebu ascendancy in Kanem, or in other words during the period of Zaghawa ascendancy.

HISTORY OF THE FIRST TWELVE YEARS OF THE REIGN OF MAI IDRIS ALOOMA.

By Imam Ahmed ibn Fartua.

IN the name of God, the Merciful, the Compassionate; may the blessing of God rest on our Lord and Prophet Muhammad, the chosen, Lord of beginnings and endings, who was sent with conquest and victory and with good tidings and warning, to all the worlds.

May the blessing of God rest on him, and peace upon his kindred, the richly endowed, the good and pure, and upon his companions and house, and those who heard his discourses—all of them.

Praise be to God who began existence with His wisdom and ordained upon mankind to follow Him, and His Prophet (may the blessing of God and peace rest on him), as fulfilling therein His reason, and completing His bliss.

Who also of intention and purpose created pairs of all things as is explained in His book that came down to advantage His creatures. Who fashioned out of water every living thing that they should trust Him, and raised them with glimpses of His love to certainty of Him.

Then, after that He had created all things, He exalted the Beni Adam, and established their position by what He fashioned. The guile of a destroyer cannot deceive Him. He distinguished for their guidance between 'the right path' and 'error' with fixed purpose—between the company of the Garden, and the company of the Fire. Inquiry must not be made as to what He is doing, and there is no comprehending His decrees—nor does a mithkal of atoms in heaven or earth escape the bounds of His knowledge. "He knows the treachery of the eye, and what the breast conceals." The issue and heart of affairs is in His hands.

M.S. Page 2. He is the first and the last, the seen and the unseen, the beginner and finisher, meet to be loved and thanked, the cause of ageing and the requiter, the giver and withholder, the director, He who abases or accepts repentance, the merciful, the mighty, the pardoner.

O my brother Muslims, God has set you and me among those who will inherit Paradise, and will dwell therein for ever; He has given you and us a refuge from the wrath of our Lord and the torture of hell. He is the hearer of prayers, Amen. There is no power nor strength save in God the most high, the most mighty. There is no God but Him, the Lord of the firmament, the generous.

Know that the cause of our engaging in this work at this time, is the perusal of the compilation of the learned Sheikh Masfarma Umr ibn Othman concerning the epoch of his Sultan, the just, despiser of the world, god-fearing, brave, and warrior king, Idris ibn 'Ali ibn Ahmad, ibn 'Othman ibn Idris, pilgrim to the sacred House of God. (May God bless his descendants and preserve his august renown till the day of the blast of the horn. Amen).

When we studied that work concerning the war in Sima describing its battles and phases, we determined to compose a similar work on the age of our Sultan, the learned, just, god-fearing, ascetic, despiser of this world, keeper of his word, the brave Haj Idris ibn 'Ali ibn Idris ibn 'Ali ibn Ahmad ibn 'Othman ibn Idris—the pilgrim to the sacred house of God, who is descended from Ume ibn 'Abd ul Jalil of the seed of Saif ibn Dthi Yazan, from the flower of the Kuraish, and the seed of Himyar. May God richly bless his successors, through the sanctity of the Lord of good tidings, Muhammad, the pure and his kindred (may God bless him and them and give them peace). He is sufficient for us and the best protector.

The Imam ul Kabir Ahmad ibn Fartua of the tribe of Muhammad ibn Mani began to compile this book on a Sunday in the month of God Rajeb, the unique, in the last third of the month, in the city called Birni.

But we did not write it to display our learning, or for appearance or effect, or in pride of spirit, but rather we employed the materials from the past we were bound to employ, working on and imitating models of the past, and noble exemplars, even though our work is poor and of no account.

God keeps our secrets, and pardons our sins. To mention His loving kindness is to give thanks, wholly to ignore it is ingratitude. Every age has its great men, and extols each of them according to his faith and works. The crown of leadership is purity in justice.

Thus every people relies on imitation of its leaders. The leader goes before and the people follow him. He leads them to the Garden as it were by a bridle, after giving them the Book of direction, glad tidings about the Faith, right direction and sure guidance in the path of the Law. So every man knows his rights and his obligations to others. Most excellent is the fame of just deeds, and justice on the part of a king for one day is equal to service of God for sixty years. Often has this been laid down. For pursuing the goal of justice the opportunities of kingship are countless.

A place where there is an evil Sultan is better than a place which has none.

The Lisan ul Arab bears witness. "I saw you running away from injustice, from this Sultan. I said, even so!"

If this is true, how about the case of a just king in whose heart is the fear of God, and who moulds his life and acts and forbearances even as God has made it easy for him to do.

M.S. Page 4. Thus we have taken in hand to narrate the mode of life of our Sultan and what he did, in a history of his reign and his wars and camps, and his clearing the roads for merchants, though we cannot pretend to give a thorough and full account of his enterprises.

For even though we were to try our very best, we should not cover more than a little of the ground and that by great effort. How can we cover the extent of his endeavour, when in one year he waged many wars. Even though a concourse of the learned in great numbers were to try to relate all his exploits, they would fail. Could they describe all his wars without omission, yet they would not know that which preceded from that which followed for certain and surely.

Our Sultan Haj Idris ibn 'Ali ibn Idris sought to follow the example of our Lord and Master Muhammad, the chosen, (may the blessing of God and peace rest on him and on all the prophets) in regard to the holy wars which the Prophet (upon whom be the blessing of God and peace) undertook; for God has guided and directed him towards making all his acts, and bearing, and endeavour follow the set road and redound to His glory.

Look how God (be He magnified and exalted) made easy his path, as we heard from our Sheikhs who have passed away, for the accomplishment of wonders and varied exploits such as no former king had wrought onwards from the days of Sultan al Haj Daud ibn Nigale, who fled to the realm of Bornu. So we will recall what we have learnt so far as we can, fail though we must, as we have already explained to you at length.

M.S. Page 5. How then about the exemplary punishment he meted out to the tribe of So, in accord with God's command to fight unbelievers, who are close to Muslims and vexatious to them.

Or again his dealings with the town of Amsaka. It is said that this "stockade" was dug before our "stockade" which Sultan 'Ali ibn Ahmad dug.

Or again his war with the people of Kano, what time they built many "stockades" in their land, seeking to harm the land of Bornu. They kept raiding and carrying off plunder, flying to their stockades and walled towns; and there hiding their gains among their own possessions.

So they did, till our Sultan attacked them with lofty purpose and aim, and destroyed all their defences except the great "stockade" called "Dala."

So also his exploits when he fought the Barbara, till the earth in its fulness became too narrow for them and the desert too small for them, so that they found no sufficient place in which to pasture their flocks or dwell.

Did he not also go to the land of Agram, and the parts of Kauwar by Amar, and the hill named "Ahanama" on which live the enemy of the race of Tubu. He killed and captured many among them, and returned victorious and happy to the town of Jawani and the town of Bulma, where he camped, and lived for some days.

The people of the land of Jawan brought him a horse as a present, in fear and submission. So they were brought before him and departed assured of his protection.

Look too at his journey to the house of God, that he might win a sure glory. Thus leaving the kingdom he loved and an envied pomp, he went East turning his back on delights and paying his debts to God (be He exalted).

So he made the pilgrimage and visited Tayiba, the Tayiba of the Prophet, the chosen one (upon whom be peace and the blessing of God), the unique, the victorious over the vicissitudes of day and night.

He was enriched by visiting the tomb of the pious Sahabe the chosen, the perfect ones (may the Lord be favourable and beneficent to them), and he bought in the noble city a house and date grove, and settled there some slaves, yearning after a plenteous reward from the Great Master.

Then he prepared to return to the kingdom of Bornu. When he reached the land called Barâk he killed all the inhabitants who were warriors. They were strong but after this became weak; they became conquered, where formerly they had been conquerors. Among the benefits which God (Most High) of His bounty and beneficence, generosity, and constancy conferred upon the Sultan was the acquisition of Turkish musketeers and numerous household slaves who became skilled in firing muskets.

Hence the Sultan was able to kill the people of Amsaka with muskets, and there was no need for other weapons, so that God gave him a great victory by reason of his superiority in arms.

Among the most surprising of his acts was the stand he took against obscenity and adultery, so that no such thing took place openly in his time. Formerly the people had been indifferent to such offences, committed openly or secretly by day or night. In fact he was a power among his people and from him came their strength.

So he wiped away the disgrace, and the face of the age was blank with astonishment. He cleared away and reformed as far as he could the known wrong doing.

To God belong the secret sins, and in His hands is direction, and prevention, and prohibition and sanction.

Owing to the Mai's noble precepts all the people had recourse to the sacred Sheria, putting aside worldly intrigue in their disputes and affairs, big or little.

From all we have heard, formerly most of the disputes were settled by the chiefs, not by the " Ulema."

M.S. Page 7. For example, he stopped wrong doing, hatred and treachery, and fighting between Muslims, in the case of the Kuburi and Kayi. They had been fighting bitterly over their respective prestige, but on the Sultan's accession, he sternly forbade them to fight till they became as brothers in God.

Then again there was his leniency in his remarkable expedition to Gamargu and Margi and Kopchi and Mishiga and to the hills of Womdiu.

He also came to the people of the hills of Zajadu and the hills of N'garasa, called N'guma, who had allied themselves with the sons of Sultan Daud and his grandsons and relatives and made raids on the land of Bornu, killing men and enslaving women and children right down to the time of our Sultan (may God ennoble him in both worlds). He scattered their host, and divided them, but of the N'guma he spared all and established them in settlements under his direction as his subjects nor did they resist or became recalcitrant.

The tribe of N'gizim, the people of Mugulum, and the people of Gamazan and others of the N'gizim stock who were neighbours were insolent and rebellious, till our Sultan went out to them with a large host, destroyed their crops, and burnt their houses in the wet season. Thus they felt the pinch of a ruined country, yielded to him obedience, and submitted to his rule.

He introduced units of measure for corn among these people by the power and might of God. The N'gizim who dwelt in the West, known as Binawa, would not desist from enslaving Muslims in their country and doing other evil and base actions. They kept seizing the walled towns of the Yedi as fortresses and places of refuge and hiding, using them as bases treacherously to attack the Muslims by day and night, without ceasing or respite. But when our Sultan ascended the throne, he and his Wazir in chief Kursu took counsel to stem the torrent of their guile and deceit, so that they left off their wickedness, and some followed the Sultan, others the Wazir Kursu, others various leaders who had waged " Holy War " with the Sultan.

To some the Sultan gave orders to settle, and devote their time to agriculture.

Again there is the record of the Sultan's dealings with the So whose home was in the East on the shores of the great lake of Chad. These people, known as Tatala, formerly perpetrated many iniquities and crimes. It is said that they took stores of water in gourds or other receptacles, and then with their weapons and shields, sallied forth to harry the towns of the Muslims, sometimes going two or three days distance on these forays.

But when the time of our Sultan came, he rebuked them with a stern rebuke, and chastised them with divers sorts of chastisement till they became downcast and ashamed. Many of their dwellings became desolate, empty, forlorn and deserted.

Know, my brethren, that in what we have told you, we have failed to tell all. We have but told you a part of the story of the deeds of the early years of our Sultan's reign, with hand and pen. How can that be easy or possible for us, considering his actions covered most of that which is ordained in the Kurá 'an and Sunna concerning " Holy War " in the path of God, seeking the noble presence of God, and His great reward.

Thus we have cut short the recital of all his wars, in this brief compilation. As for his wars on the tribe of Bulala we will—please God—relate the Sultan's dealings with them in a separate work plainly and clearly and accurately, according to the accounts obtained, and following all the descriptions which have been given of the wars which our Sultan brought to an end by the might and power of God.

We have here desired to follow the descriptions of the expeditions of our Sultan, al Haj Idris ibn 'Ali ibn Idris with the events that attach to them approaching them chapter by chapter from the affair of the So N'gafata to that of the So Tatala; making clear distinctions—if God wills—so that he who attends may learn the truth about the chief events, and the manner in which our Sultan made war upon his foes, by what stratagems he fought them, and by what guile he destroyed them: in what array he advanced to victory over them all, and discomfited them.

Thus we will follow the path we have indicated—if God wills—in this book according to all we have seen and heard. To God, belongs perfect knowledge and bounteous wisdom. After we have finished this our appreciation, we will write—God (exalted be He) willing—of that which concerns the affairs of the land of Kanem with chapters on the fighting that occurred as we saw it and recollect it from our marches and journeys, even as the learned Sheikh Masfarma Umr ibn Othman wrote of what he knew of the age of his Sultan Idris ibn 'Ali ibn Ahmad.

We have ceased to doubt that our Sultan al Haj Idris ibn 'Ali accomplished much more than his grandfather. God willing, we will shortly make plain how he visited Kanem in our book devoted to his exploits there, so that none who reads can doubt, by the help of our Lord (be He exalted), and His beneficence and design; for He suffices for us, and is our best support.

There is no power or strength except in God, most high, most mighty.

But now we must return to the story of the So N'gafata, whose doings we have mentioned above. So also we will write of the affairs of all the peoples we have mentioned in due order and sequence just as we set them out at the beginning of this book.

M.S. Page 11. Know that as concerning the acts of children, and those of their fathers and grandfathers of old who have gone before, there are three possibilities. There are children who recall the deeds of their sires and surpass them by far, clearly and without question. There are children who fall away from the examples set by their fathers in an extraordinary way. There are again those whose deeds are like those of their sires, and neither surpass theirs nor fall short, but are as like is to like or as the fashion of one sandal is to its fellow.

In the first place God (be He exalted) has showered kindness on His slave—the writer—and given him a rich guerdon and help, even as He declares in His book the Kurá'an, in the stories of the prophets and others (upon whom be blessing and peace) in a way that tongue cannot tell.

We have seen that the deeds of the Sultan (may God on high enrich His bounty with plenteous beneficence and favour) were such that if an account of this era were narrated and set forth, we should never hear the like recorded of the reign of any of our former kings.

May God increase our Sultan's might, and excellent renown and peace, so as ever to grow onward to the days of his posterity to the end of time.

Anyone whose claims to greatness in comparison with his sires, were as the claim of our Sultan would have just cause for pride. It is no mere theory that he surpasses them all and has no peer, exalted above them in his wise counsel, and prompt action.

Did not Ibn Doreid in his book say:—

" Of all that a young man gets, you get a share
" There remains to a mortal after his life the beauty of
" renown.
" Corresponding to a man's words when he is alive
" Is the memory of him when dead. The fame of the
" man of Understanding is fair."

So it is. Our Sultan the Amir ul Muminin and Khalifa of the Lord of the worlds, who visited the two noble sacred cities Sultan Idris ibn 'Ali, ibn Idris (may God ennoble him in both worlds), sought to attack his enemies the So N'gafata, and destroy and scatter them. He therefore built the big town near Damasak and put Shetima Biri Getirama in command, together with his son Ajima Gasma ibn Biri. He made four gates in the town and placed a keeper in charge of each gate—and quartered there a detachment of his army. He ordered all his chiefs who were powerful and possessed of a defence force, to build houses, and leave part of their equipment there as for instance, the horses, and quilted-armour for them and coats of mail.

After he had done this he gave the town the name of Sansana ul Kabir. The people who lived in it were strenuous fighters in " Holy War ". They went out morning and evening, seeking the enemy, fending them off, until God designed the ruin of their towns.

The Sultan again built another town to the North of Birni near Sansana and South of it. It was a large town. He placed there Chikama Buma, and made two gates only, the Eastern gate and the Western gate and no more.

He handed over to Chikama Buma many slaves of the Kardı so that by reason of their numbers there was little room.

Chikama and his slaves continually sought out their enemies the N'gafata morning and evening without weariness, or remission or quarrels or failure. So they continued till God rent the covering of the heathen, and destroyed their wicked towns.

When our Sultan had finished building the two above mentioned towns, he turned his thoughts toward a policy of cutting off root and branch these evil doers.

He sent forth a crier among all his people ordering them to come to him with matchets and leather shields and weapons and plentiful provisions, saying that no one must remain behind either of the Ulema or herdsmen or merchants. His aim was to cut down the trees South and North that the unbelievers would have no place of refuge left, and could not find means of hiding from him, saving the weak who could not fend for themselves, such as infirm old men, and the sick and women.

Thus he ordered criers to proclaim in every market in Bornu that the people should come to him prepared and ready to complete his purpose.

M.S. Page 14. They heard and obeyed, and worked together as he wished. When the news of this spread and reached the heathen, they assembled. Their people who had come under the protection of the Sultan and agreed to pay the customary ' poll tax ' broke their agreements. They tried to stop the trees being cut down and drew up their host for war.

The Sultan was indifferent to their host, and came on with his army of horse and foot, until he reached their trees and towns.

This was in the hot season. Picked shield-bearers were drawn up in front of our army in companies. There stood behind them the horsemen clothed in mail, with quilted coats as armour on their horses. They were in compact array and in companies.

Then the Sultan chose people with matchets to come up behind the horsemen and cut the trees. They were stout of heart steeled against the hurts and evil of the unbelievers. With them were dancers with a company of minstrels playing on viols and drums and horns and flutes, and various other kinds of entertainment; all designed to strengthen the bodies of the Sultan's people who were engaged in cutting the trees, and make them eager and quick, and oblivious of home-going.

When the Muslims were formed up in this surprising array,

pursuing this unusual plan, the enemy charged down on them with bows and arrows and spears.

Fighting went on for a long time, but God (exalted be He), gave the Muslims endurance, and made their footsteps firm, so that the enemy were unable to prevent them from cutting the trees. Praise be to God, the unique, the victorious.

Now when the time of the rains came, and the corn put forth its shoots and sprung up and was good to look on, and almost ripe, the Sultan, the Amir ul Muminin Haj Idris (may God ennoble him) went out with his army, and cut the corn of the enemy, leaving none at all.

The Sultan continued these three policies, cutting the trees in the hot weather, cutting the corn in the rains, and raiding the enemy in the cold season, till it became very difficult for them to stay in their walled towns. They deserted the denuded areas and moved elsewhere.

In the following year when the time for the cutting of trees came round, the Sultan Haj Idris, in accord with his custom, came to cut the trees at the town of Maya. The heathen assembled with their hearts full of anger, and fought a fierce battle with the Muslims, and succeeded in making them desist.

The Muslims returned to the place of their midday halt, and the heathen were delighted on that day, in that their trees were not cut.

They hoped and believed that for the future their successful fight would advantage them, and so returned to their ill deeds.

When the Muslims returned to their halting place, the Sultan was angry with them, very angry, and asked how did this occur? They saw that their Sultan was displeased, and his wrath lay heavy upon them. So when God brought the morning, they advanced towards the town of the enemy to cut the trees.

The unbelievers hastened to drive them back trying to do as they had done the day before. They charged the Muslims—a horrid host. But the Muslims cared not, but pursued their tree cutting.

Then the enemy attacked on all sides, and, divided into many parties, charged the Muslims. But it did them no good. The Muslim horsemen and the archers from the West crept up under Wazir Kursu.

> Lo there has been gathered for them
> As it were a showing up of their affairs:
> My detractors have assembled, and their hurts reach me.

The shield-bearers and all the chiefs put forth their utmost endeavour and cut the trees, and did not return till the day was well advanced.

Thus they cut the trees on the second and third days, till there were no more trees left at Maya and Badama. In a few days they reached Charmu.

The Muslims were astonished at the cutting of the trees of Badama in such a short time, and the enemy were entirely nonplussed.

The Sultan then divided up his armies, and ordered every section to return to their quarters and clear their farms until the proper time for cutting trees or spoiling farms or deeds as mentioned above, came round.

Then the enemy experienced the pinch of the three kinds of pressure upon them. They gave up burying corn, except for those whose farms were surrounded by deep pools on every side.

M.S. Page 17. Thus the Sultan's victory over the first of the unbelievers was assured. The faithful triumphed—the amirs, and officers and their followers and horsemen—in that means of feeding their children was denied to the enemy, and every man in Bornu hoped for the destruction of their towns.

No one had dreamt of such a thing before Sultan al Haj Idris ibn 'Ali, who carried out the design, hoping that his Lord (be He exalted) would fulfil his task and make it easier for him.

His Lord (on high) had indeed chosen him, and made him excel in wonderful resource and fruitful design. There was no rivalry or competition with him on the part of the people of his age. They followed him taking example from the injunctions of the Hadiths and Kurá'an.

No one great or small among the Muslims, or among the pagans, ever expected the destruction of all these thickets. Thus the enemy were deceived and came to the great town of Sansana twice to attack the Sultan. The first time they retreated without a battle, for the Lord (be He exalted and His perfection glorified), cast terror into the hearts of the dirty idolators. They returned a second time and a battle took place.

M.S. Page 18. God put to flight their host in accord with the promise in His spoken word. They broke and fled whence they came.

The Muslims followed them vigorously, killing and wounding: leaving their corpses strewn like the branches of a stripped palm tree. The Sultan ceased not hemming them in, and cutting off the remnant of their advance by day and night with his slaves and freemen. So when they were hard pressed, they came in great numbers to the Sultan, reduced by stress, subdued, penitent, and yielding. They said: "We are your slaves, who "will serve you, even as your own slaves, who obey your every "behest; who call ' labaika ' and live where you choose."

The Sultan camped at Damasak and told the Imam ul Kabir Ahmad (the writer) to write down the names of all these people. So they came to him, and he wrote them all down one by one and completed the list.

The Sultan with his sure skill and exact thought made a new plan and ready device like his former one, wise ruler as he was, by the power of God (be He exalted). He divided his host and sent some against the town of Dabushka, some against the town N'gazar, and some against Zimbam. Thus he scattered his men urging them towards the borders of the enemy.

Then he returned to the cutting of the remaining trees reducing the thickets, so far as God (exalted be He), intended, and he gave orders to the army to return to their homes—that is to say those who had scattered in the land after the Sultan set forth on the Holy War. They departed to their valleys, except those leaders, and chiefs, and henchmen who never left the Sultan in any circumstances, morning or evening. So these remained with him after the departure of all the rest of the people. Thence the Sultan proceeded with them to the town of Kabulu, or rather near to it. There he divided the leaders and chiefs, and sent Kaigama Muhammad Kadai, that is to say, Abd ul Kadim with the Arabs to the town of Dabushka on a Saturday to fight the heathen N'gafata.

M.S. Page 19.

He sent Hirima Ibrahim with his people to the town Zimbam and sent Mulima Abd ul 'Lahi Afunu with his force to N'gazar to fight the enemy on a Saturday. He sent Yerima Gote and his men to Bidu Guru, and Chikama Muhammad ibn Fargama and his people to Gamaka to fight the enemy who were North of the river. He ordered them all to fight the enemy at the places to which they were sent: more particularly to attack on Saturday and not put the attack off to another day.

Each of them went to his appointed place on a Thursday. Then after the Sultan had done as we have narrated, he came to Kabulu and prayed there the Friday prayer.

After the last prayer in the evening, he set forth with his soldiers at dead of night to the East towards the town of Mamuka.

M.S. Page 20.

At daybreak prayer time he was close to Mamuka. He dismounted and prayed the morning prayer; then mounted, and attacked the unbelievers of Mamuka fiercely and suddenly. None escaped save those who hour was not come. After their destruction he turned his bridle North, and went on till he dismounted at the town of Damasek in the morning on his return.

All his captains who had been sent to attack the heathen at different points, did as they were ordered: they gave battle on the Saturday as did the Amir ul Muminin on his part. Evil was the morning for the admonished, and evil the end of the unbelievers.

Such is the policy of those kings whom God has set to uphold the right and remove evil, who follow the book of God (be He exalted), the ordainer, and the practice of His noble Prophet upon whom with his relations be excellent blessing and peace.

So in this straight path Sultan al Haj Idris rooted out the enemy among the So N'gafata, and cleared the kingdom of Bornu of them, and followed the precepts of our Prophet and Apostle Muhammad (may the blessing of God be upon him and peace) even as the Sahabe before him and their successors followed them.

M.S. Page 21. To gain a strict observance of the Kurá'an and the Sunna he turned over all disputes to the learned judges, and put off his own shoulders onto theirs all manner of judgments. May the Lord of the worlds reward him in both.

Let us return to our story. The greater number of trees of the enemy which we cut to the South lay between the river at the town of Kasidon and the town of Kirki and the town of Badua. To the North we cut from the river at the towns of N'gatua and Dagambi to the towns of Diba and Kwakwa. All that region was full of the enemy, the pagan N'gafata. They never ceased injuring the land of Bornu for a day, according to their nature, till the epoch of the rule of our Sultan al Haj Idris. May God ennoble him in both worlds, and make easy for him the destruction of his enemies the N'gafata on every side.

When he encamped at the town Badruga in his advance after his well known fashion cutting the thickets with his whole army of horse and foot and shieldmen and archers and gunmen and axe-bearers and others—a numerous host—his men set to work cutting and carried on for a few days.

When on the Wednesday he sought to send back the army to their quarters, he ordered the chiefs and leaders to attack the tribe of Gidama on every side.

Reign of Mai Idris Alooma of Bornu. 21

So they slaughtered them till the number of slain could not be reckoned.

When the Sultan returned to Bornu from one of his raids in Kano, he came and encamped at Runi in the morning, and spent the rest of the day there. In the evening he marched with his army to the East to look for the enemy who were in the plain of Sansana the great, to slaughter them and clear that part of the country of them.

M.S. Page 22.

He subdued them by the power and strength of God, catching a great number of them unawares. Not one escaped through hearing news of his approach. They were killed to the last man.

A man called Baya who was an envoy between them and the Muslims was killed. Their retreat was cut off, and they were encompassed to such an extent, that they scattered among the Bornu villages of the tribe of Tura and other tribes to save their lives. When the Sultan heard the news of this he sent his amirs and captains to look for them in the villages and ordered them to kill all they found.

They did so. So the enemy knew that the land of Bornu was closed upon them: and that they could not find in it a resting place or retreat. So the enemy fled again to their remaining cities, Bikadwa and others in the East.

Then the Sultan came out against them, and the Muslims as before cut down their trees. They raided them. The guides and the first horsemen reached the enemy, and slew those they found unprepared, so that they fled and entered their walled towns. Then the rear of the army advanced, and the Sultan encamped at the town of Bikadwa.

M.S. Page 23.

The Muslims assembled and went in search of the houses of the enemy so as to convert them into houses for the Muslims as a protection against the eyes of men, and the wind, and heat of the sun.

The enemy began burning their houses with their own hands from that time to forestall the Muslims burning them. Terror took hold on their hearts even as is written in the Book sent down from the Lord of the worlds. An evil fear mastered them, and a quaking stupefaction, so that they could not distinguish between a male and a female camel, or a sheep and a bull, or a she-goat and he-goat, or any goat or sheep or ram.

They lost count of the days and months and time. The Sultan then arose, and divided his host according to his former practice. It was his wonderful plan to order the people of Sansana al Kabir to advance towards the pagans on a given day as if to battle. But in reality this was a stratagem and they had no such purpose. They just left the town for the far bush with no intention of fighting, but to let the Sultan get between the pagans, and their towns and so defeat them.

M.S. Page 24. They heard the Sultan's order and obeyed, and made ready as if for battle and came on as instructed. The pagans came out from their towns towards our men, whereon our men pretended to fly. The pagans followed them into the bush. When the pagans got close to the people of Sansana, the latter gave way to draw them on to the Sultan who lay in wait for them. The pagans did not suspect this stratagem at all. So they remained, until the Amir ul Muminin Haj Idris arose from the town of Gaiawa in the early morning and marched against them, cautiously, taking the lower road which leads past the town, so that he could pass between the town and his men.

Thus he marched with his army. When he got close to the town, the people of Sansana saw the dust rising up, and charged the enemy a deadly charge, in delight at the arrival of the Sultan.

When the sinners saw the dust of the Sultan behind them, rising up to the sky, they knew it must be him to a certainty, so they turned their backs in flight, seeking the city for safety. The Sultan and his force hovered between them and the city.

On that day which God (exalted be He) made a day of victory for the Sultan, none escaped, not even the Zindik who was the envoy between the Sultan and the pagans, namely Muhammad ibn Magua. He was killed among the last of his people flying towards the town. The Sultan won a great victory and all the Muslims were delighted.

M.S. Page 25. They returned to Sansana at nightfall. Look at this wonderful planning and rare stratagem on the part of this clever captain and noble Shah.

So the Sultan continued his course by day and night till the enemy were hard pressed in the city and country. Thus they continued. Then, so we have been reliably informed, the slaves of the Sultan who lived at Sansan Kerde, who carried shields, and were footsoldiers, not horsemen, covering their bodies with leaves, and were wont to brush aside the rushes of the heathen, awaited their oncoming and attack. When they found a man, they killed him out of hand, but the women and children they enslaved and kept them alive for sale.

It is said that, when the slaves of the Sultan raid the pagan country in the night when all are asleep and at rest, in order that capture may be easy, the pagans are so sunk in oblivion, that rising is difficult. They lose their wits, and their bellies are like their backs from dire hunger.

In this case they remained, until they got into the direst straits. So when the year came, in which God (the glorious and mighty) in His purpose designed to expel them from their towns, there came the Amir ul Muminin and Khalifa of the Lord of the worlds, al Haj Idris ibn 'Ali with his whole army, even as the pagans had made common counsel to attack him. He camped at the town Bitukur or near to it. The Muslims set to work to cut down the remaining thickets, and the enemy all tried to stop them but were unable.

M.S. Page 26.

They spent all day on their feet and alert, trying means to circumvent the Sultan. Then they assembled all their people, and took counsel, and determined to charge the Muslims in a body at night, when the latter were asleep.

At dead of night when all our people were reposing in sleep and all was still and silent, they came in great numbers from the East, and made a raid, and wounded some of those they found. But only the people in the threatened quarter were disturbed. All other parts of the camp were undisturbed, and cared nothing for their coming and their idea that they would be successful at night.

When the pagans saw that such was the case, they returned on their tracks.

In the morning the Sultan and his army followed them up. When the forces came within sight of one another, the Muslims charged the enemy, whereon they fled without stopping and entered their town.

The Sultan passed on to the town of the tribe Duguti and killed the proud and wrongdoers among them.

After that all the N'gafata town dwellers fled, so that there were none left. They went to their brethren, our enemies, the So Tatala and dwelt with them and built houses there, and remained a little time.

M.S. Page 27.

When the rainy season came on, they moved towards Bornu to commit harmful and treacherous acts. When the rains were over, they went back to the Tatala. So they continued coming and going between the Tatala and Bornu.

When our Sultan perceived what they were about, he led his army in the direction of the Tatala, waiting on their tracks. They saw that the Sultan would not leave them in this region. They were afraid, so they collected their belongings and all fled to the region of Mandara. They took up their abode between Mandara and the land of the Gamargu, founding a town and settling.

When the great king, Haj Idris ibn 'Ali, the glorious, whom, may God ennoble in both worlds, heard news of this town, he prepared for war and marched to Mandara. He found the N'gafata there.

He slaughtered an innumerable number of them—the number is known to God alone—so that their dwelling became a waste and desert.

The Sultan and his army returned to Bornu with much booty in great joy.

After this expedition these heathen no longer lived in swamps. Some went to Kanem, namely the tribe of Duguti, who, however, were not a large tribe.

M.S. Page 28. This is what we knew of the story of the N'gafata. No one remembers all that occurred between them and the Sultan. Therefore we have abbreviated the full story taking into account its fullness or scantiness.

To God (on high) be all praise, the Lord and giver of victory.

Now we will return to narrate the story of the land of Amsaka, by the will of God, most exalted, and His purpose.

The people of Amsaka were not of one tribe. They were a mixed people of different kinds. They had no single chief. They built a stockade to the East of the land of Mandara, and surrounded their stockade with a deep ditch, and were insolent, rebellious and very troublesome.

They had been like this for a long time, and no one thought of trying to stay their evil courses or hoped to do so. They did not weary or abate from doing damage constantly. We have heard from reliable sources that Kaigama ibn Burze and Sultan 'Ali of Yamta used to make expeditions together against all the towns of the heathen except the land of Amsaka alone. The only reason they held off and left it alone was because of the power of its inhabitants in war and their stout defence of their town.

Such had been the position in olden days even before the stockade of Sultan 'Ali ibn Ahmad was built.

When the age of our Sultan Idris (may God ennoble him in both worlds) came, he marvelled at the character of this town of Amsaka; at its stubbornness and exclusiveness and presumption.

By the mercy of the most generous he came to Amsaka with the chief of Yamta to see its character, the wiles of the people and their array and resistance. He came up to the stockade and went round it, and made an attack suddenly as a reconnaissance. There was fierce fighting between the Muslims and the inhabitants, but the attack was repulsed.

The Sultan accordingly drew off for the time, and returned home with his army. So also the chief of Yamta went to his town.

For a few years the Sultan kept the matter in his heart so as to give it wise consideration. Then when the time of their destruction which God (most exalted) had written for them in the guarded books came, he picketed his horses at Ganka after the well known fashion, to feed them up and put flesh onto them.

Then the time came to leave Ganka. So the horses left their place of picketing, and passed by, and went a few days' march.

The Sultan left Ganka in the month of God Rejeb, the unique, after the afternoon and evening prayers. After sunset he went to the region of the town of Lada, the region of gathering together of the army, and original trysting place.

The Sultan encamped there on the morning of Monday, and slept there two nights. The whole army met him there, coming from every side of the country.

He set forth against the heathen of the tribe of Tatala, and on his march passed through people of the land of Tawati, who were unprepared for attack. He slew them all, and none escaped except those who had left on a journey, or those whose hour was not yet come.

Then the Sultan left the country of the Tatala and came towards the region of Amsaka. He pushed on with his army a few days until he reached the town of Kasa. Thence he came to Sangaya which is close to Amsaka.

In the morning the Sultan arose with his army and arrived before Amsaka about 9 o'clock. When the people of the town saw the dust of the Muslims rising to the sky, they mounted onto the tops of their houses and the pinnacles of the walls to observe what the Muslims would do.

The Muslims showed their intention. When the soldiers saw the idolaters and heathen observing them, they wished to charge forthwith upon them.

But the Sultan stopped them from going forward, and ordered them to be patient and restrained. Then he passed by the edge of the stockade opposite the town, and crossed to the South and camped by the East gate about the distance of a short gallop on a "maidan." When the camp had settled down the people piled their gear and saddles and slept till the morning.

The people of Amsaka grew even more contumacious and stiff-necked and obdurate, and began shouting in their delight and joy, and cared not at all for the presence of the Sultan and his army threatening them.

M.S. Page 31. They were misled by the result of the former fierce engagement and the strength of their stockade. It is said that in their pride and self sufficiency they said to the Muslims:—

"You are as you were before, and we are as we were "at first—and neither side will change—and none save the "birds will see the inside of our stockade and town."

Thus they spoke to our people. Then came the Amir ul Muminin to their stockade to attack them in force. The enemy mounted above the stockade, and fired arrows and darts like heavy rain. No Muslim could pause a moment in the vicinity of the stockade without being pelted with arrows and hard stones which broke a man's head if they hit it. The stockade was full of people.

The Sultan ordered the Muslims to fill in the trench which encircled the stockade with the stalks of guinea-corn which the pagans had planted for food. They tried this plan for two or three days, but whenever the Muslims returned to their quarters in the evening, the enemy came out and took out of the trench all the stalks that they had put in it, so that nothing was left. This went on for some time. The Sultan then commanded the whole army to move and encamp close to the stockade to the North. They did so. This fighting took place in the month of God Sha'aban.

M.S. Page 32. The Muslims came to try and fill up the trench of the stockade in the early morning after they had shifted camp close to the town. Horns were blown and flutes sounded. There was all manner of noise and playing in the stockade.

The pagans set themselves to attack the Muslims in every possible way, and to divert them from the ditch by all kinds of wiles and devices; firstly by setting fire to thatched roofs, and throwing them down—a most formidable device; by poisoned arrows; by pots of boiling ordure, or throwing hard clay which would split or break a man's head; then by throwing short spears, or finally by throwing the long spear which is carried by warriors.

All these were among their methods of fighting. They never ceased day or night. One day a section of the stockade, about the length of a spear was broken down. The Muslims thought they would gain entrance through it and follow on. But the pagans built up the place with mud in the open, the Muslims looking on and unable to prevent them building.

The Sultan then ordered the army to cut tall trees to make platforms on three sides of the stockade, so that the gunmen could mount on them and easily shoot at the enemy inside the town in every direction possible.

They did as they were ordered. The people then worked with a will in filling the ditch of the stockade with earth as well as corn-stalks, and continued obediently till they had filled the ditch with earth.

The place became flat and even. Then our men began destroying and breaking up the stockade itself with matchets and axes until they had cleared a large amount of the stockade away, and so the enemy were hemmed in.

To the Amir ul Muminin and Khalifa of the Lord of the worlds, al Haj Idris ibn 'Ali (may God most exalted ennoble him in both worlds) belongs the credit for an apt device and clever plan by which to fight the enemy—to wit, his order to the army of the Muslims that the gunmen should get in the first discharge so that they should not be forestalled. Thus the enemy's hands would be rendered empty and victory over them would be easy. Thus it fell out. The pagans began to shoot at the Muslims with showers of arrows but our army picked up all their shafts and took them to the Amir in great numbers. It was impossible to count the number of arrows collected. God alone knows. Finally the arrows of the enemy came to an end. Nothing was left.

The heathen therefore assembled all their blacksmiths, and asked their help in making arrows. The Muslims outside the stockade heard the noise of beating of hammers on the big anvils which are placed in the ground (*i.e.*, with a stump fixed in the ground) for the making of new arrows.

The enemy then began shooting with new arrows, covered with mud in place of the former poison just to frighten the Muslims pretending they had poison on them though it was not the case.

The Muslims continued to destroy the stockade with matchets and axes, and filled the ditch, except that they left on the West side a part which they were unable to fill. After a time they destroyed the Eastern part of the stockade, leaving a part in the middle. The enemy then became afraid, and lost their heads, in terror and fright.

The day wore on. It grew hot. Then evening came. It was a Saturday (4th December, 1575) the last day of Sha'aban. After sunset the new moon of Ramadan came out and the people saw it. The Sultan prayed the evening prayer and refused to leave the battle. He ordered his tent to be brought, and slept among his troops. He directed the big drum to be beaten in a changing rhythm, to put fear into the hearts of the pagans.

God cast into their hearts exceeding terror and a great dread. So they remained in fear and trembling, and ran from their stockade under cover of darkness.

The Sultan followed them, killing the men and taking alive the women and children tracking them down and following far without let or delay, so that none escaped among the heathen save a few.

M.S. Page 35. The Muslims all returned in the belly of the night, safe, with booty, joyful at the enemy's discomfiture, save one man known as Ajima ibn Kalle. He became a martyr in the confusion at night (may God pardon him). That night the Muslims all slept with purpose to keep the fast on the morrow.

On the succeeding Thursday morning, the Sultan ordered his people to cut the trees inside the stockade. They cut them leaving nothing of them. Many of the enemy were slaughtered in the stockade. The stench of the corpses of the slain grew unbearable in our camp. The Sultan ordered his men to gather together the captives into one place. When they were assembled he ordered his Kerde slaves to kill them all. They killed them. No one was left alive.

Then he gave the word to march. The drum was beaten, and he left Amsaka at the head of the army, after there had happened and been brought to light all that has been here related concerning this rebellious and stiff-necked people. It has been published to the four quarters of heaven, so that near and far could hear of the power of our ruler, and commander, and king.

The people of every quarter came to him with many gifts bowing their heads in submission whoever they were or wherever they dwelt.

So there was destroyed this stockade which held out against 'Ali ibn Idris' predecessors. He turned upon it and rendered it barren and deserted.

The people who brought presents continued to pay the poll-tax as of old every year, and became more and more obedient. The Muslims who were present know all that we have related.

M.S. Page 36.

Such is the story we have learned of the fighting at Amsaka, and the deeds of our great Sultan al Haj Idris (may God ennoble him in both worlds).

We cannot record all that happened, for as we have told you before, we are unequal to it and unable—unable to recount all the events, occasions, and circumstances.

When Sultan Idris left Amsaka with his army, he went West in pursuit of his enemies among the Gamargu. The people did not know, however. He concealed his purpose. The Muslims thought he was returning to Bornu, and nothing else, and went on marching. But after passing Mandara, he made a night march pressing on with all speed his forces, and reached Bahewa in the Gamargu country. The people were reposing all unprepared. The Sultan slew them, and captured their children and wives. No one knows the number of slain and captives save God most high.

We have heard from a trustworthy source that none of the Sultans—the Sultan Yamta or Sultan Mulgai or Sultan of Mandara—attacked the Gamargu in the open. They always concealed their attacks, hoping to catch the Gamargu unprepared.

M.S. Page 37.

If they knew that the enemy had perceived them and were prepared, they returned and fled until the night came. Then the Gamargu would come up with the attackers and inflict loss on them.

Such was the usual event when the Sultans attacked the Gamargu. The saying goes that in the land of the Gamargu the hawk does not attack the chickens because they are so numerous and their arrows are poisoned—so it is said allegorically.

Our Sultan Haj Idris encamped in the morning with his army of Muslims, but he cared nought for the stockade or numbers of the Gamargu.

Our men spent the day, and slept there.

On Monday they arose and hunted the Gamargu, but saw no one, for the latter had fled for their lives and left the battle field deserted.

The Sultan went in the direction of Marghi, then returned and marched in the direction of Bornu till he came to the great city Bumi Data.

There the army dispersed and went to their homes with gladness and joy at the booty they had obtained.

It behoves us to make mention of the affairs of the land of Kano by the command of Him who, if he wish, saith " Be " and it is.

M.S. Page 38. When the people of the land of Kano sought to bring evil and damage on the land of Bornu, they began a new policy which did not obtain in the days of their forefathers at all. They built a large number of stockades. One of them was a stockade in the land of Kazra, the second at Kelmasana, the third at Majia, the fourth at Ukluya, the fifth, a stockade called Dulu, the sixth Auzaki, the seventh Ajiyajia, the eighth Sayaiya: the ninth big stockade was called Galaki, and there were others the names of which we do not know.

Among them was also the walled town called Kai. Our commander Haj Idris gave orders that the trees of Kai should be cut down. They were cut down with a will, by might and main, just as those of the stockades we have mentioned. It was because the people of Kano wished to do mischief and evil, and to injure Bornu treacherously, that they built the stockades which we have described.

They kept on raiding Bornu and then flying to their nearest stockades with what they had filched from the Muslims and concealed, before the pursuers from Bornu could reach them. They got back without being overtaken.

Such was the kind of treachery they practised on all the borders of Islam, coming and going between the two countries continually.

M.S. Page 39. Then our great Sultan al Haj Idris rose against their evil deeds, and treacherous designs. He evolved an apt plan to destroy all their stockades, and sought the counsel of the army upon it They agreed to the plan.

So he ordered them to prepare. They obtained axes and matchets and all tools for cutting and destroying. Having obtained them they set out for Kano.

They began by destroying the stockade of Majia. When the Sultan and Muslims drew near to the town, the inhabitants began to discharge clouds of arrows and made a fierce resistance. The Sultan ordered the gunmen to fire a volley at the enemy. They did so at once. The pagans turned their backs in flight and fled to the bush in the night. The Muslims pursued them and took some property and those fugitives who were infirm. Victorious they returned with their booty and destroyed the town.

Majia was blotted out and became a barren plain or empty desert. When they returned they saw in the deserted stockade many corpses and dead animals strewn about.

The Sultan ordered his army to march elsewhere to another stockade. So the drum was beaten, and they marched to all the stockades, the names of which we have mentioned, and found them all deserted.

The Kano people scattered pell mell when they heard about Majia and what had been done to it by the Muslims. The army resolved to destroy all the stockades and carried out their resolve so that none was left in the land of Kano.

M.S. Page 40.

Great joy filled the hearts of the people of Bornu, that God made easy for them the destruction of the rest of those stockades without fighting or fatigue or toil, and that none of the new stockades which had been made for treacherous purposes, remained. Nay they were as clouds of dust or things of yesterday save for the stockade of Dala.

The people of Kano became downcast in the present and fearful for the future, concerning that which was in the foreknowledge of God only, meet to be praised and glorified.

The people of Bornu made many raids upon Kano, particularly the raid of Majagani.

Such is the account we have had of the deeds of our Sultan Haj Idris ibn 'Ali and the fighting between him and the people of Kano as our poor understanding has grasped it. May God, the hearer of prayers and bringer of hopes to fruition, ennoble him in both worlds.

We will now set forth the war between Haj Idris and the Tuwareg who had attacked the Fellata. They were wicked doers and robbers, who wrought ill to the Muslims, and did evil on the earth.

M.S. Page 41.

They did not act justly, but harried the Fellata by night and day, when they least expected them.

We will mention the methods the Sultan employed to avert this trouble and fend off their harmful and stubborn treachery, till he forced them to repentance, and gave the Muslims rest and deliverance and peace.

Our Sultan Haj Idris made three attacks on the Tuwareg in person, when God granted to him a great slaughter of his enemies, not counting the expeditions of his captains and amirs and others among his people such as the tribe of Kileti. After these expeditions the Barbar were downcast and sought virtue. Of the three expeditions we have mentioned, the first was called Siktala or Butiras, the second was against the Dankir or Targi-aga, and the third took place between the country of Ahir and the country of Tadis.

When our Sultan, the Amir ul Muminin, went out to prepare for the expedition to Siktala, the inhabitants ran away taking their women and children and goods into the desert far away. The Sultan followed their tracks, caught them up in the evening, and killed nine of their most famous warriors.

M.S. Page 42. We have heard that these nine in their valour and prowess would not brook defeat, and had sworn by God (most great) that they would never give way alive.

So we had heard concerning them before they were killed. Then God (be He exalted) smote them of his goodness and favour, with a great fear and terror when our Sultan attacked them and they fled from their land. But their flight availed them not. They perished in one spot, so that none could dispute it. They were even as the nine men of the people of the prophet Salih (upon whom be peace) whom God mentions in His great book.

After the Sultan had slain these nine, he took their wives and children and goods and returned to Bornu with his army, safe: victorious with booty and joyful.

The amirs and captains too gained what was given them by the Sultan, a fifth of the booty.

As for the expedition against the tribe of Dankir, the Sultan set out against them, after making ready, from the town of Kulia or Lastera, and reached their abode after a march of two days.

M.S. Page 43. He came in contact with the enemy in the morning. They chose to fight with their shields (dark). The Muslims charged them fiercely from two sides, South and North, and broke into their ranks, and came out behind.

They then broke and fled, the Muslim army following, killing and beating them down with their weapons. None knows the number of slain save God most high.

The Muslims received no hurt, save that one man, a Turk, called Ali Ghar, was killed. The Sultan then returned and halted at midday to rest, with his booty, victorious and glad and happy. He divided the booty in the midst of their town; a severe humiliation to them and abasement to their devils, bringing joy to the hearts of the Muslims, even as in various passages of the Kurá'an which relate to what is permitted or authorised.

The Sultan was intent on the clear path laid down by the Kurá'an and Sunna and the words of the wise, in all his affairs and actions. He never went outside the sanctions of these three guides to conduct, or shunned, or avoided their obligations. All his people knew that such was his character and no chronicler of his age would doubt it. As an indication of his excellent qualities, is the innovation he made in building a mosque of clay. Formerly the mosque was of thatch, but he planned and saw that there was a better and more correct form. He destroyed all the old mosques in the Birni, and built new ones of clay, knowing how to hasten in the cause of the Faith, as is laid down in the Kurá'an and Hadiths. He sought nothing thereby but a heavenly reward, from the mighty Lord. Again, he devised boats to help the Muslims and make it easy to cross the river in a short time and in comfort.

M.S. Page 44.

In ancient days, a boat was on the model of the hollowed out drinking troughs, with which shepherds are wont to water their flocks and herds—a contrivance called in the Bornu language "Gagara."

If a Sultan wanted to cross the river with his army, it took him two days to do so or three days, even though the ferry men and polers did their best to get them over with all speed.

But when the age of our Sultan Haj Idris came, he discarded these "Gagara" and made big boats, so that the people crossed the river rapidly and were carried in large numbers by one boat.

Thus the Sultan arranged and planned for the benefit of the camels and horses and baggage of his army so as to lighten the trouble of the march. Formerly most of the transport of the army was droves of oxen and ponies and mules and donkeys. No one then had many camels. Hence travelling in the waterless places was difficult for them.

M.S. Page 45.

But the Sultan Haj Idris ordered his amirs and captains and chiefs and all, who were able, to buy camels, to make easy travelling in his reign, since it was trying and difficult as has been related.

So ingenious, clever, masterful and able was he. Had it not been for these arrangements, the march to Agram and the country of Dirku had not been easy for the amirs. In many other ways his ability was wonderful. We have mentioned a very little, passing over much in fear of being lengthy and verbose. But the sensible reader will understand that beyond the port there is a big sea.

M.S. Page 46. We will now complete the first part of the story of the war against the Barbar. Our Sultan al Haj Idris ibn 'Ali marched from Atrabisa in Kutushi to the land of the Barbar, he and his army, and crossed the country of Gamaram (Damarghu) constantly ready and prepared for a fight.

He found most of the people of Ahir in the open desert between Teldas and Ahir. Their stragglers were killed. None escaped save him whose day had not come. Then he returned, marching, till he halted at the town of Zibdu and then came to Susubaki. At the latter he stayed a few days. Then he returned to the towns of Munyo and Kileri, and stayed there a few days. He then returned to Bornu.

All the three expeditions took place in one year. Before the fighting took place the Tuwareg including part of the Teluz and other big clans sent challenging the Sultan to come out and fight them. He was at Kasimwa, but would not go himself, as he despised them and was contemptuous of their power. So he remained at Kasimwa, and sent the Wazir Kursu ul Kabir at the head of the Muslim army with orders to use some ruse and attack them.

M.S. Page 47. A battle took place between the army and the Barabar, at a place called Agalawa. It was a fiery engagement. The Tuwareg stood for a time, but fled defeated. The Muslim army followed them, and killed many of the Tuwareg. God only knows how many. None of the Muslims were killed except the slave Nasr ibn Sakali. The Muslims took much booty, camels, slaves, and weapons, and were full of joy.

They were in the midst of their rejoicing over their victory at this place, when, lo, their commander came, and ordered all the tribe of Kileti who were there, to make raids on the land of the Barbar constantly day and night, so that the latter would leave the land of Bornu and go far away into the desert.

When the people heard these orders of the Sultan, they turned and made raids morning and night and drove them away by their fierce attacks—far away. The Tuwareg grew dispirited at their losses in men and beasts and wished that there had never been any war between them and the Muslims.

When their losses of beasts grew heavy and grievous they sought peace from the Muslims humbly, so that their flocks should not be all destroyed.

So peace was made between the Tuwareg and the Sultan, who gave them leave to return whence they had come. They returned. He did this in obedience to the precepts of the Book of Truth, trusting in God, the Creator.

Some of the people of the Barbar became the vassals of the Sultan, and gave up their allegiance to the king of Ahir and ignored him. They had followed him at first, but now they left him altogether.

Such is what we remember of our Sultan's dealings with the Barbar, as witness God most high, who brings to pass, by His kindness and favour.

We will now recount the affairs of the chief of Marghi Magaya. The chief of Marghi was called Adwa. He had been accustomed to follow our Sultan in war just as did the other amirs of Bornu. This had gone on for some time, but Adwa then refused to follow the Sultan, and rebelled in his pride and threw off his allegiance altogether.

Every time the Sultan ordered him to come, he took pains to keep away. So the Sultan went to look for him and marched to Kopchi and the rock of Mishiga and the rock of Womdiu, where Adwa's chief wife called Gumsu was found with all the provisions she had stored.

After he had put a stop to the wiles and treachery of this Marghi chief, the Sultan returned, and camped at the old city.

Then the chief of Marghi came to Birni N'gazargamu in person, and sat in abject submission before the Sultan, throwing dust on his head with his two hands, entirely humble and overcome.

In the same way our Sultan dealt with the defeated Amir of Mandara. The latter had turned out and deposed and driven away his nephew. The deposed monarch came to the Sultan as a refuge seeking help and assistance from him against his wicked uncle, who had snatched away his kingdom. He was given a robe of honour, and regained his kingdom in accordance with his father's expressed wish to the Sultan which was thus carried out after his death.

The origin of the affair, so we have heard, was as follows:—The deposed king, who came to the Sultan for help, had been nominated by his father. The latter was afraid of his own brother and what he and his followers might do after his death. He was afraid that they would be unfaithful to him.

The Sultan accepted the dying injunction of the king. So when matters turned out as was feared, and the deposed monarch came to him, the Sultan made preparation and went in person with his army to the city of Kerawa.

When its inhabitants saw the Muslim host advancing by day, they fled defeated with their wicked king to the big wide hill, which is West of Kerawa, and climbed to the top, so that it was impossible for the Muslim army to attack them or get at them. So well fortified were they.

M.S. Page 50. The Sultan returned home; but when the next year came round, he set out to catch the wicked one, he and his people. They found the Mandara people on the top of the rock as the first year. Then our Sultan Haj Idris formed a good and certain plan at a long spur of the hill which he invested, so that want and hunger overcame the enemy.

They saw that the end was certain, so became afraid and came down from the top of the hill.

When they came to the place of audience, the Sultan's heart relented and his wrath was appeased, since God had accomplished his purpose and showed him bounteous favour.

The Muslims were delighted. The Sultan restored the deposed king to his throne.

Look, my brethren, at what this Sultan our Sultan Haj Idris did, how he accomplished the dying injunction of an unbeliever after his death. Again, look at his benefits to and compassion towards the Muslims, without any favouritism or preference of one over another. Nay, he divided his favours so equally that none could ever say another was preferred.

Such was our Sultan's method and policy always. May God establish his throne even to his sons and grandsons till the blowing of the horn. May God ennoble him in both worlds and give him highest happiness.

We have already mentioned one of his journeys to many places in the Gamargu country and Marghi and Kopchi and Mishiga and Womdiu in search of the ruler of Marghi.

He made this journey to hem him in and compel him to return into a constricted area.

M.S. Page 51. It has now occurred to us to mention the affairs of N'gamazan and of the people of the town of Mugulum and the people of Daura of the tribe of N'gizim.

Having numerous champions they grew headstrong and rebellious and began wickedly to raid the Fellata. Such had been their conduct from of old.

But they did not distinguish between the different races, and raided all alike. So when the Sultan heard this and their wickedness spread abroad, he set out against them with men and provisions at the time when their corn was up.

The army cut their corn leaving none at all. The Sultan continued to destroy all their crops including cotton and simsim. A few years passed, and every year they were treated thus, and in one day there was destroyed all that it had taken them a long time to grow.

There is no greater hardship for an enemy than the destruction of his crops. Hence in his wise counsel the Sultan tried it.

We have heard that the Wazir Kursu ibn Harun marched with his numerous army to Mugulum and invested it in the blackness of night.

He slew and captured many and returned. An ill fate had overtaken the inhabitants so terrible that no description is adequate to record it. But in spite of that and the cutting of their supplies every year regularly they were not deterred from their evil courses.

But when the Sultan attacked them with his full forces they became submissive and abject, and became as his slaves who measured out corn as tribute every year. This is what we have heard concerning the N'gizim whom we have mentioned, and the war with them in the time of our Amir al Haj Idris (may God ennoble him in both worlds).

And now (by the might and power of God) we will pass on and mention the affair of the tribe of N'gizim in the West, called Binawa. As far as we can gather the tribe of the N'gizim in the West called Binawa were more difficult than the people of N'gamazan and Mugulum, and Daura, because they had a more intimate acquaintance with Muslims, and because of their very wicked acts.

They knew the whole country intimately themselves and had no need to use spies or scouts. They spent the day or slept where they liked in the Muslim country, and did not care.

After these excursions they would leave either in parties or singly and seek the leader whom they had appointed to be their confidant in crime and wrong doing, with whom they worked in collusion, and under whose direction they operated even in the middle of the land of Bornu.

Concerning the war with these Binawa in the time of Sultan Abd ul Lahi ibn Dunama we have heard that their chief called Gamaru, and his warriors, harried the Fellata, and made raids in

M.S. Page 52.

the day time from the town of N'gamzan towards the West, and returned unafraid and confident.

Now at that time the Sultan of Bornu was living in the town of Kitle, and his officer Kulima Duma ibn Haruna was to the North of the river, and his officer Fuguma Abdullahi ibn Fuguma was to the South and was acting for the Sultan.

A chief was thus posted on either side, but the Binawa, the inhabitants of those parts, took no heed of them and set themselves to stop the roads, and cut off Bornu from the land of Fali so that none could go by night from East to West or even from West to East.

If people wished to journey from East to West, they had to go round to the North and make a long detour, then return towards their destination. This everyone was obliged to do, merchants and others, few or many, at the time the Binawa trouble was at its height.

It was impossible for Muslims to pass along the recognised roads, till the time of our Sultan Haj Idris ibn 'Ali (may his Lord ennoble him and make easy for him his purpose). When he became ruler over the land of Bornu, it was not long before the chief of the Binawa by name Gamaru came and submitted and became a Muslim. There also became a Muslim after him one Nasar called Bultu with a few of his people.

Most of the Binawa, however, did not become Muslims, fearing their deep guilt and the evil of their sins and actions so recent and near to the age of our Sultan. Their leader Gamaru died soon after he became a Muslim.

Nasar called Bultu came to the Wazir ul Kabir Kursu, and remained with him becoming a good Muslim. When Bultu was established as a regular counsellor of the Wazir, the Wazir sought his advice concerning a plan to overcome and make himself master of the Binawa who still did evil deeds.

When Bultu heard such counsel from the Wazir he was much surprised and came to him. "Since you ask my advice about this" said he, "though I am an N'gizim and you belong to the same race, the matter is light and easy, if God, exalted be He, wills."

So they agreed to go out together. The Wazir set out with Nasar, and they camped at a place where there were shallow wells and trees. Here he sought out the Binawa who were raiding in the bush. All that came in to him he made to swear that they would follow him only, swearing them on the most noble Kura'an in regular fashion if they recognised its binding power. As regards doubters, he guided them gently into the right path.

Thus he dealt with them, and thus all the raiders turned away from their evil courses—even the man called Farsasku—and became entirely well-behaved.

Some of them became Muslim soldiers, others became merchants. God made safe the road between East and West, and everyone followed the regular road without making detours. Brigandage ceased. Thus much we know concerning the affairs of the tribe of Binawa, and have recorded to the best of our ability and recollection.

But God suffices for us, and is our surest stay.

Among the wondrous acts of our Sultan Haj Idris, is the way he destroyed four enemy strongholds. One of them was the town of Mawa, the second the town of Agham, thirdly the town of Bani, and fourthly the town of N'gajimbana. Each of these was fortified with a wall of great strength and their inhabitants were N'gizim.

They were rebellious and stubborn, and did many evil and wicked actions. They had a false idea of their own strength by reason of two things. Firstly their numerous archers, who used poisoned arrows, and secondly the strength of their walled towns. These two factors induced them to be rebellious and hostile, as has always been the case with the heathen, and there was no concealment about the fact.

M.S. Page 55.

But when our Sultan Haj Idris ibn 'Ali observed their wicked rebellious acts, he made up his mind to go to the town of Mawa, after celebrating the 'Id ul Fitr in the town of Mugulum.

The reason that he came to Mugulum for the 'Id was as follows: He had been camped at the town of Kasimwa for some time, and then had marched with his army, and rested at Gaiawa.

On the morning after he came to Gaiawa, he with his army had marched on and camped at Kaburuwa, and thence had gone on marching South till he reached Marguba. He slept at Marguba for two nights or three, and then went forward and camped at the town of Disi, and thence marched to Mawa and camped.

From Mawa he moved to Gija Gijami, and thence without halt he came to the town of Fika and camped there. On this journey Sultan Haj Idris visited the wonderful water called Jinjina, after crossing Fika country. He returned from there towards Sade going West. He reached Sade in a few days and attacked it.

The people with him got much booty, and plunder. The

Sultan then led his army to the North, and reached Lere, and Abula and N'gamazan, and Mugulum.

M.S. Page 56. He camped with his army on the second of Ramadan (of great power) and remained making raids and capturing slaves till the end of the month.

He celebrated the 'Id ul Fitr at Mugulum, and the above account shows how he came to do so.

Let us now return to the story of the N'gizim.

After celebrating the 'Id at Mugulum, Sultan Haj Idris did not rest, but passed on with his army to Mawa, after sending his prisoners to Bornu.

He paused on his march a whole day, and camped in the bush. We reached Mawa with him at about 9 o'clock on Monday morning. When our army got near the town of Mawa, the inhabitants began to attack us boldly, being ignorant of our power and badly deceived. Had they known how invincible we were, they had never come out of their town.

The Muslims caught the enemy unprepared and the two forces met. The enemy pelted our men with darts and arrows without ceasing. They pressed upon them with missiles hotly and fiercely

But our people stood firm. The gunmen opened on the enemy with a volley, and poured a hot fire into them before they had time to array themselves or make ready their defences. When they saw their plight, the enemy turned their backs and fled to their town in haste. Our men followed them up, and surrounded the town from all four sides. Then the unbelievers were amazed, and their sense of discretion left them. Their retreat to their town was cut off, while if they went in the reverse direction it availed them not, since the fire of war had been kindled.

M.S. Page 57. All who were hit by gun fire died, even the animals and oxen and horses. The oxen then rushed out wild with panic. Each time they made a rush, our people drove oxen to their quarters, taking them for their own as booty. This joyful occupation continued, till the town was emptied of all its cattle.

As regards the women and little children, some ran outside the town like the cattle.

The men on the other hand split into two parties. Some stayed near the gate or opposite to it, fighting on till they were killed by gunshot instantaneously, as if they had drunk poison.

How fierce was the fire of the guns! All whom they hit were mortally wounded and died, their members broken. Thus all the leading warriors were killed in this place as soon as they came forward.

The cowards and weak kept in the background, and concealed themselves so that the gunmen should not see them and kill them as they had killed the brave among them.

They waited for nightfall with the women and children who were left. As Ibn Yakut says in his laudatory work:—

"Their brave men drank destruction,
"Their cowards were encompassed by bounds and
"deserts!"

The cowards thus waited for the darkness of the night, and sat tight in the town till dark when the fighting finished. When the Muslims wished to return and disperse to their camps, the chief scout Idris ibn Juma'á objected. At that time the office of Wazir was filled by his elder brother Kursu ibn Haruna. The people obeyed the injunction of the chief scout and agreed to wait near the town for the coming out of the enemy.

In the late evening, out they came with their women and children from the gate, running away. When the Muslim army saw them in that plight, they charged them fiercely—one shock only—whereupon the men were the first to run. The women and children scattered. They were seized as captives and booty. Our people kept on capturing and leading them away till no more were left to capture. Very few of the women and children escaped.

The whole army was glad and rejoiced exceedingly over the affair and took it as a good omen for the conquest of the rest of the towns. They returned at night to their camp, and slept for the rest of the night in joy and gladness.

In the morning the Sultan told his army to advance. They advanced. He led them in the direction of the town of Agham, and pitched camp there before midday. As soon as he arrived he ordered the royal trumpeter called Mulima Nasar to call the people by trumpet call. Nasar immediately carried out the order. There assembled the horsemen, and shield-bearers, in haste and in great numbers. There was no hanging back except that the weak who were totally unfit for service, remained behind.

Thence the Muslims moved on to the town where were the enemy. The army was quickly drawn up for battle. When the Agham pagans saw the Muslims, they went into their town intending to resist. They seized their weapons and shot poisoned arrows.

The gunmen, however, made things hot for them, and broke them by their fire.

M.S. Page 59. They then turned and fled. Most of them were killed. Some, however, were fortunate enough to escape by flight to the town of Agham. The Muslims captured their women and children as slaves. Agham was treated as the town of Mawa was treated.

Our warriors returned to their camp before sunset joyful for they had not the trouble which they had at Mawa in making captures at night. Here they had a peaceful night's sleep. When the morning came, they were ordered to go forward by beat of the big drum. They hastened to get under way. The Sultan marched with his army to the West and did not stop, till he reached the town of Bani before midday.

When the heathen of that place saw the Muslims encamping they would not come out of their town to fight. They had heard of the fate of the people of Mawa, what time they advanced to repel the attacking army, and failed to do so. Nay—they were conquered and humbled and their noses rubbed in the dust. They were like a prudent man who is fighting desperately with another. They stayed in their town, and stood to arms, with their poisoned arrows.

When the Muslims saw their tactics, they made ready for battle. All the shield-bearers and musketeers advanced towards the town, getting quite near.

The pagans then let loose a fire of arrows as thick as a cloud of locusts or like a rain storm. But the Muslims were undismayed, relying on the constant care of the Lord, most beneficent, and His goodness in helping their Sultan, and giving him victory of the two towns beforetime, Mawa and Agham.

As regards the chief, the energetic Idris ibn Haruna we saw no one to compare with him in his conduct of the attack in this town.

M.S. Page 60. His plan of campaign was as follows: He sent forward the shieldmen, in front of him, and placed the musketeers behind them. He then took up a position with his horsemen by the side of the musketeers or behind them facing the town but not going up to it, so that he should not have any casualties. His men continued to advance and the pagans to shrink back. When the fighting became too hot for the pagans, they retired into a narrow place in the town where no one could see them. There they hid with their weapons in their hands, waiting for night in order to fly, as the people of Mawa had done.

Then the great warrior Idris ibn Haruna halted in accordance with his old practice, as he had done in his fight with the town of Mawa, and waited his opportunity.

When the sinners began to use night as covering and means of getting away, the Muslims sought means of stopping them, since they got tired of waiting for their coming out in order to fall on them. The two armies remained there till nightfall.

The pagans and their women and children who had not been captured prepared for flight to a safe place. But the Muslims heard them moving and, assembling in the midst of the town, prepared for them with firm resolve and stern purpose. So when they came out pell mell men and women, the Muslims fell on them fiercely, and pressed them sorely. The enemy host scattered. Our men followed them killing the males, and capturing their wives and children.

Few of the pagans escaped; just those whose time was not yet come, or those whom God most high saved in His providence, as He had predetermined. The women and children of the enemy slept that night as booty.

None of the Muslims were hurt save one man, namely Barbuma ibn Abdulahi of the Magumi Milima. When we woke in the morning by the command of God and His decree, be He exalted, the Sultan al Haj Idris ibn 'Ali (may God ennoble him in this world and the next) gave the signal for marching in the usual way by beat of drum, towards the town of N'gajimbana. **M.S. Page 61.**

The people mounted. The Sultan followed the road and marched with them, and reached N'gajimbana which is a strong town bigger than Mawa and Bani.

The town of Agham also is of very wide extent, but as regards strength of stockade and defences, N'gajimbana is stronger than Agham, if God wills, for He is all-knowing.

When our Sultan came up to N'gajimbana with his army, and sought to attack it and reconnoitre, God (most exalted) of His favour and grace, divided the counsels of the enemy, so that they split into two parties, each following a chief, and each upsetting the counsels of the other party. One party wished to follow without fighting or strife, the others wished to fight to the last.

Fierce disputing arose on either side, and the peace party came out of the town with their women and children, and went to a place far from the town and sat down there. But those who were hostile and held back, remained with their leader in the town intending to fight.

M.S. Page 62.

We have heard that on that day the warriors of the enemy smeared their bodies with dirt and filth as an antidote against the guns, and that in this condition they entered the fight against our men who were trying to enter the town.

Our leader, however, arranged his shield-bearers and musketeers as was his wont in past battles. We never saw Muslim fight as that day our leader fought. In this town he fought with an even greater fury than he did in the case of Mawa, and Agham and Bani.

The unbelievers of N'gajimbana thought they were more warlike than the people of Mawa and Agham and Bani, and that their arrows were more deadly than the arrows of the rest. But their wickedness and iniquity deceived them. Had it not been so, they had never sought battle with our Sultan, after the inhabitants of the town had divided into two parties.

Under these circumstances our leader excelled in doughty deeds and deeds of prowess, pressing on to take the town in front.

The pagans were drawn up in ranks in the midst of the town and pelted the Muslims with darts and arrows.

Our leader ordered the shield-bearers to tie on their shields and stand motionless, and the musketeers to fire on the heathen and press them with a heavy fire without ceasing.

Our soldiers used all their skill and courage in the fight, without resting a moment.

We have heard that the leader of the enemy, he who was at the head of the polytheists, wished to lay in wait for the great leader Idris ibn Haruna and trap him by stealth. Thus he did not shoot at anyone else, but prowled round to catch the Wazir unawares to shoot him, relying on his prowess and full of vanity and conceit.

M.S. Page 63.

The leader Idris understood only too well, or better than he, what he was doing, and the difference between a clear front and a handful of men sent out as a bait.

God helped the Wazir. His section stood firm and shot at the enemy, and took their leader prisoner. The Sultan then put him to death, and the Muslims took much booty. They celebrated the occasion with great thankfulness and joy.

The news of the victory spread to all the towns of the land of Gugaí, and the land of Katagum and other N'gizim towns. They came in and followed the Sultan, giving up rebellion and resistance.

The Sultan returned to his city (Birni) with his armies,

joyful and victorious. He remained only a year or two in Bornu, before he went on a pilgrimage to the sacred house of God. May God accept his journey and greatly ennoble him in both worlds, through the grace of our prince and master, Muhammad, and his kin. May the blessing of God rest on him and them and peace.

We must now return and relate what befell between the tribe of Tatala and our Sultan Haj Idris ibn 'Ali (may our Lord ennoble him in both worlds).

The tribe of Tatala were obdurate and stiff-necked people. They vaunted their shining white spears, and paid heed to no other weapons at all. They thought themselves the most wily and cunning pagans, for their custom was to charge down upon people when they were asleep or unprepared, and so rush them and undo them. No pagans were more dastardly than they. The greatest boast among them, so we have heard, is to have killed a good man.

When they meet together to feast, if there is among them a man who had not killed a Muslim, they at once expel him with contempt, or make him eat of the feast alone, and do not share it with him. Such was their ancient habit down to the time of our Sultan al Haj Idris ibn 'Ali, may his Lord ennoble him, and his benefactor give him felicity.

M.S. Page 64.

When Idris became Amir by the favour and mercy and beneficence and purpose of God, he took counsel how he should put an end to these iniquities, and adopted a fine new plan, an idea which would settle the matter.

It largely consisted in building camps near the pagans, and settling Muslims in their vicinity, so as to allow them little empty country.

Secondly, constant attacks on their territory in the hot season and the winter so that they got no rest.

Thirdly, cutting down their crops in the wet season.

Fourthly, he kept falling on the tribe of Kotoko, enveloping them with many boats when they were unprepared, killing some and capturing others.

Thus matters went on till the pagans became very weak. Before the age of our Sultan, they used to wander about in the land of Bornu. They wandered so far that they reached the towns of Magiburum and Maba.

Idris stopped all this. They were unable for a single day to cross the boundary and come into the middle of Bornu, fearing the Sultan who had so signally supported the Muslims and settled the pagans, fearing that he might meet them in the bush, and slay them.

Thus they ceased leaving their villages, and were obliged to stay near Lake Chad. When the waters of the Lake receded East, they crept after them, taking their huts with them to the edge of the Lake, to save their lives. They did this as if the Lake were a fortified **city.**

M.S. Page 65. Then the Amir ul Muminin (may God prolong his might and enhance his victories), marched one day with his army to the town of Sabi and, finding the inhabitants there, slaughtered them.

He marched on another day to the town of Kansa Kusgu, reaching it about two o'clock. Many of the inhabitants were slain or captured.

I remember that when Sultan Haj Idris had finished destroying the farms of the N'gizim of the town N'gamazan, he divided his army into two portions, placing Kaigama Muhammad Kadai in charge of one portion, and giving him the greater part of the army with orders to proceed South till he came to the town of Tagalaga, in the territory of the N'guma, and to reach there by Sunday at latest, without fail, and have entered the town by that day.

The Amir with his captains and army took a more northerly route, and reached the land of Tawati on the Sunday about 2 o'clock at the same time as the Kaigama with his captains reached Tagalaga.

They slaughtered all their enemies in these two towns. None save God, most high, knows the number of the slain. And God filled the hearts of those whom it was decreed should escape with exceeding terror, and cowardly fear. Thus they fled scattered.

Many gathered in flight towards the edge of Lake Chad, fearing for their lives the whole time.

Thus the whole country of our enemies the Tatala remained in fear and terror so that many of the villages became deserted, and want came to them.

Again the Sultan the Amir ul Muminin Haj Idris ibn 'Ali (may God prolong his life, and establish him victorious), camped one day at the town of Mara. There came to him the chief of Mafati with many boats. Each boat had many of our foes confined in it.

Idris had them turned out, and handed over to the Muslim soldiers who slaughtered them to a man. He ordered his slave, the chamberlain, called Saba to attend to the enemy of the town of Kansa Kusku, and take up position near the town to attack it.

So the soldiers waited there with Saba a short time. Now each host was afraid of the other, and guarded its position and ground. When night came, the chamberlain ordered his men to approach the enemy when they were asleep, that God might decide as He willed between the two hosts, in His foreknowledge.

Such was the plan agreed upon, complete and final.

Children prefer people who are like their parents in character and acts, just as slaves prefer one who is like their master. The lack of resemblance between the two hosts described, was astounding.

The Muslims struck camp and went to Kansa Kusku by night. When they got near, they held off, awaiting the pagans awakening from sleep at sunrise. When their enemies woke they had no knowledge at all of the presence of the Muslim army in their country, and rose as they were accustomed to do.

The chamberlain and his army charged down upon them fiercely, without pause or stay. They began to slaughter the pagans with their various weapons, spears and so on. The pagans then fled, after a long stand, to the region of Lake Chad in panic to save their lives.

The Muslims with their leader the chamberlain, did not rest from pursuit, slaying the males and capturing the women and children in large numbers. A few of the pagans by the will and purpose of God, most high, escaped. Thus their light failed and their dwellings were destroyed, and became empty and void, just as was also the fate of the people of the town of Sai. They scattered to the towns of the pagans in the South and no cultivated spot was left in those two places.

When the news of these two events spread abroad and reached the towns of the Tatala, they loathed having to stand it, and refused to face it. They moved away to the shores of Lake Chad and dwelt there, fearing the raids of the Muslims. Fear continued to dominate them till they were in sorry plight and poor. They began to give up their wonted practices, their greed, their evil doing, and the wicked excesses which they were used to commit in Bornu, wandering about the country.

They left off these practices taking warning from the fate of their brethren and took refuge in two remedies, but for which they would all have perished.

In the first place they ceased penetrating far into Bornu as formerly. In the second they suffered to decay the dwellings which their ancestors had built and moved to Lake Chad as we have already narrated.

A sensible enemy is better than a foolish friend, as Salih ibn Abd ul Kudus says, where he formulates his wise sayings in verse:

" Man gathers together: and time scatters:
" He is raised aloft, and misfortune tears his fortune to
    " shreds.
" It is better for him to be the enemy of a sensible man,
" Than for him to have a foolish friend."

Thus it is. As for all our Sultan's acts and plans during his reign, and his comprehensive wisdom and judgment with regard to the Tatala and other enemies, he based his conduct on the book of his Lord, which sets forth every kind of judgment, and on the Sunna of His prophet (upon whom be the greatest blessing and peace), and on the sayings of the learned of olden time, who deduced their judgments from complete sources and the fruit of understanding; and on those of their companions and their followers and those who followed them and came after them, the rightly directed, with all of whom may God be pleased.

We will give all details in the story of the Tatala.

M.S. Page 68. When the Sultan Haj Idris son of 'Ali had settled the people of the land of Tawati he lead his army East and camped at the town of Busugwa.

At this town the enemy raided the Muslims by stealth and killed some people, but the Sultan took no notice of them at all. He returned to the land of Tawati and camped there. He stayed there a few days and thence marched to Gagadu Kusi where he remained some time. All this was during one month of Safar. The Sultan did this to cow the enemy and sap their strength.

This tribe of the Tatala had aforetime made large and extensive settlements between South and North. They extended from the region of Sabi to the region of N'gala and Mongonu. All these people were fugitives. They included those who had left their houses for good and settled in other towns; those who had migrated to the borders of the Lake; those who were sojourners without women; and those who had lost their children and property. They went about in terror. The earth was too narrow for them, as we have described before.

The Amir ul Muminin had built many houses called Sansana near these pagans to stop them coming into the land of the Muslims by night.

He placed in each Sansana many soldiers who would be able to fight the enemy independently as occasion arose. When the Sultan initiated this plan the visits of the enemy to the Muslim territory became few. With the cutting of the roads, their opportunities for ill-doing as they were wont, were cut also.

So they despaired of the possibility of ill-doing and became afraid for their lives, thankful to save them, which was a greater boon than they expected. People were greatly surprised at the Tatala; at their softness after their hardness; at their quietness after their boasting.

So they remained our enemies morning and night. May God not take away their fear and humility forever and anon while the ages pass.

Such is the story we have learnt of the relations between them and our Sultan Haj Idris ibn 'Ali (may his Lord exalt him on his throne). God is our stay and sure trust, and He is the accomplisher for His slave the poor and humble.

Then the Sultan, the Amir ul Muminin and Khalifa of the Lord of the worlds, so we know, had fierce fights with the tribe of Makari save in the case of the town of Kusuri and the town of Sabalgutu.

The chief of Kusuri, whom we have mentioned, came out with his army but was captured alive. By capturing him the Sultan gained a great victory.

As regards Sabalgutu, the chief and people did evil in their city, and were full of insolence, and wickedness.

When our Sultan, the commander of Islam, heard of it, he settled matters completely with his army, crossing over into the land of Mandara. When he arrived at the town battle was prepared. The enemy came out and drew up in ranks. But as soon as the Imam began to attack them, God cast into their hearts, great terror and vile cowardice. So they broke and fled from their town. Many of these heathen were slain, and their women and children captured.

The Muslims gained a great victory, and took much booty. They were exceedingly glad and took the booty as a good omen for the journey which was ahead. They sent all the booty they had taken towards the region of the city of Bornu, being weary and tired, when lo! their journey did not end in these valleys. On the contrary they went over and marched against the tribe of Mandara.

They reached them in a few days, and were as successful as they had been with Sabalgutu (by the help of God, most high, and His assistance).

The Muslims suffered no loss in penetrating these two towns. The Sultan returned with his army safe, enriched, victorious and happy.

Wake O my brethren! Listen O fortunate people! Our Sultan Haj Idris, may God prolong his victories and make easy his path, was chosen by God for many good purposes and deeds. Though his word might be great or small, he kept it. Did he promise, he fulfilled his promise. Did he propose to do some painful thing to anyone, that person, if sincere, felt no anger, since he knew the character of the Amir. Did he reward anyone, he never did a petty action nor did he swagger before any of God's creatures.

He devoted his talents to the service of God, and entrusted his affairs to the foreknowledge of God, were the issues sweet or bitter. He was not dismayed by adversity and misfortune, nor was he browbeaten by evil doers, did he know their evil doing.

He did not rate the things of this world higher than those of the next. He knew that this world was transitory and would cease to exist, and that the next would endure and remain forever.

He did not put off the times of prayer.

Even though he were pressed and busy, he was immensely generous, compassionate to orphans and widows, and the poor, constant in endeavour to improve his country, and impatient of its hurts.

Were it his duty to do a favour, he did it, as to the Amir of Mandara, when he came to him in trouble, when his paternal uncle had driven him from the throne, and worsted him.

M.S. Page 71. So the Sultan tried to restore him to his kingdom, and did not cease going and coming between Mandara and Bornu, till he had ousted the unjust usurper from power, and abased him. He raised up his suitor into his rightful place, and gave him back his kingdom without trouble or contention, and returned with the now defeated usurper to Bornu, for fear he should return to his evil ways. God then made easy for the Amir of Mandara his affairs. He crushed the froward and rebellious among his chiefs and others, composed their differences and made peace.

As an example of the fine character of our Sultan Haj Idris, may God exalt him in both worlds, he left Birni on the 27th of Ramadan for the West, and halted at the town of Mara. He made the afternoon and evening prayers there, and then passed South marching rapidly. It was in the rains.

When he was close to Diskam, the rain came down heavily, and the Sultan observed that certain sections of his troops wished to enter the town; but he passed on without stopping, even though he was soaked.

The people continued tired and wet; their clothes and saddles were soaked; till they reached the town of Dagazabi in the evening.

They were then bound to fast, but the people broke the fast owing to thirst, and did not wait for night.

The Sultan then mounted and his people with him. They crossed the river (Komadugu Gana) near the town of N'gazar and journeyed the whole night pressing on till the morning. By afternoon they reached the town of Alaraba. The Sultan then launched forays South and North. They did not return till late the next morning capturing some prisoners. The Sultan returned to N'gazar and camped there before the approach of evening.

The people slept, weary and thoroughly exhausted, and prayed the evening prayer—hungry. It was impossible for the Imam Ahmad ibn Sofia that night to pray the Ramadan prayers with his Sultan by reason of his fatigue and faintness, for the march was a cruel one. When the time came to praise the Lord in the morning, the Amir ul Muminin Haj Idris mounted with the army and marched to the big city, the Birni. They had not yet reached it when they saw the new moon of the month Shawwal.

M.S. Page 72.

They entered the city between sunset and 8 o'clock and slept there. The drum was beaten for the 'Id ul Fitr.

After this wonderful march, when the Sultan visited the country of N'gazare, and after his return from the heathen country of Marghi, our Sultan marched again to N'gazare, and camped at the town of Zimbam by moonlight on the 12th of the month. When the night grew dark, the Sultan and his men mounted continuing their march. Their guide through the night was Salih ibn Kusani. He went in front of the army slowly without excitement or flurry. We shall not forget his guidance (if God wills, be He exalted) on that night. When we reached the big tree which is near the path—which is known as Kiltau—a long halt was called lest the pagans should hear the clatter of the army near them. When daylight came to guide the army, they were in sandy country. They prepared for battle and put on their accoutrements and the quilted armour of their horses and charged down on the heathen. The enemy were quite unprepared, for they had no news of the Muslims and had not seen a single horseman among the host.

In that hour the pagans were wiped out. Some escaped as their hour had not yet come, some were killed as it had come. The Muslims took many women and children.

M.S. Page 73. The Sultan found most of the pagan boys at the place of circumcision. They did not run away.

Idris then returned to Zimbam. He and his army came to the river. Thus did he return from his warlike expeditions to the West. Coming to the town of Jaba, he slept there. He then, when it was still night, set off South in the direction of the N'gizim tribe, leaving the road to Bornu (Birni). He reached the land of those pagans. Some were killed or taken prisoners. He then turned his bridle towards Bornu.

Thus he proceeded looking for a man called Dawa, son of the slave of God, the chief of the town of Bulugi. The Sultan's slave Diris al Daf found him and killed him. Very many of his people were captured.

There were many expeditions like this. We have not recounted a fourth nor yet a fifth of them. Our shortcomings and forgetfulness are evident and plain; our inadvertences are many and obvious. Yes! Yes!!

Forgetfulness may be defined as forgetting something which we once knew, and not remembering circumstances; inadvertence as mixing up one thing with another.

So we saw in a recent work, a compilation called " *Wa Lilahi Durru* " by Busîri.

" I do not appreciate your writing according to its length.
" Words may run to great length—and come to an end."

But all things return to God. God is sufficient for us and our sure stay.

O people! If you believe the deeds of our Sultan in war and Jihad, his expeditions, and hold them in remembrance, tell us the number of them and how they were conducted!

M.S. Page 74. We have written what we know. Our Lord (be He praised and exalted) has assisted and strengthened him to stand firm, fastidious concerning the affairs of this world and the next, nobly and with distinction, without failure or falling away. May God fulfil for him his reward in both worlds for He will not spoil the reward of those who do good.

We have looked in the books of the foundations of the law, as regards the number of the wars of our master Muhammad (may the blessing of God and peace be upon him). The wars are shown to be twenty-seven in number. The first of them was the war of Waddan, the last of them the war of Tebuk, which was waged in the summer. We have seen in the book Masari 'u'l 'Ashâk, that 'Ali ibn abi Talib did not take part in a single one of these wars except that of Tebuk. In going to Tebuk he disobeyed the command of the Prophet (upon whom be thanksgiving and peace), who had told him to remain at home as his deputy; may God be pleased with him.

In regard to the character of our Sultan, the Amir ul Muminin Haj Idris ibn 'Ali (may the Lord ennoble him and endow him with excellence), God laid upon him the obligation to wage Holy War and raid, as a special favour from Him (be He exalted), and gave him good hope of heavenly reward. He did not choose this world in preference to the next, when he had any affair in hand and took counsel and thought. If he found a precedent in the Kurá'an or Hadiths upon which the four rightly directed Imams who have gone before agreed, he did it following the example of those who had gone before; if he did not find any precedent in the Kurá'an or traditions, he would leave off, and turn aside from his course altogether.

Such were his two lines of action. He kept no secrets from those in whom he reposed confidence. As regards this, if he was upon a journey and heard any news of the enemy by night or day, he did not rest but went forth among his people to the source of the news with the army following him; leading himself for fear any misfortune should befall which he was able to avoid, or by his power to save. He relied on his Lord in everything and God was his support, sure that nothing would happen except by the foreknowledge of God (be He exalted). Hence he was a brave warrior who advanced everywhere, appearing promptly without pausing or beating round, until what he proposed was accomplished. Such was his character and his disposition.

M.S. Page 75.

Among the gifts with which God had endowed him, was an impressive appearance. All his followers, small or great, never felt contented except in his presence. Even though he sent large armies in one direction and went in some other direction with a small force himself, his captains were not content to go without him, however large the number of the army.

Thus whatever journey he undertook himself with a small force, leaving the large numbers to go by some other route, they would not agree to remain with the people apart from him. Their hearts did not rest being in a dilemma between the two courses, until God joined them again to their king. (May God give him great victory). We know this by testing it in many different fields.

O people! Where were you at the fight on Friday in the town of Sima when our people were at their wits end until God gave them a great victory, and there was general rejoicing when their Sultan came to them.

Sultan Adbul Jelil, the son of Abdul Jelil of the tribe of Bulala, came to Sima to war with a small army. A fierce fight ensued. People's hearts were in their throats. Then the Amir al Muminin Haj Idris ibn 'Ali, came to them at nine o'clock on a Thursday in their distress. The enemy were broken and fled like donkeys running away from a hyena. Thus were the Bulala terrified at seeing the dust of the king to the East of them going up to the sky. The Sultan (may God exalt his powers and make his victory great) followed them far, till the horses and mounts grew weary.

As the Poet said:
"I marched by night, until their horses were tired
"Until their war horses were too weary to be led by the "bridle."

He returned in the evening. Had God not favoured the host of Bornu, He had not helped them by sending to them the king, even as He helped the host of our lord and master and Prophet, Muhammad the chosen, (may God's blessing rest on him and peace), on the day of Sisaban by the hand of his nephew and son-in-law Haidara, our lord and master 'Ali ibn Abi Ṭalib (may God most high be pleased with him). Had it not been for the Sultan misfortune had happened. So he brought joy to the hearts of the men of Bornu and he made their eyes cool. So they congratulated each other and fell on each other's necks on the Thursday, and Friday and Saturday.

The king gave them robes of gladness in accordance with the universal joy. He then returned to Bornu.

Such is the story we have heard about this Thursday and the fight that took place on the third of the month Shawwal. This was one of the remarkable achievements of our Sultan and with this was the fact that the horses which he left behind him when he went to war were much more numerous than those which he took with him. The same was the case with pack animals. The shields were all left at home and were not sent after him.

Reign of Mai Idris Alooma of Bornu.

Such was his policy and his method, with which God had endowed him from birth. There is the saying, "To God belongs all wisdom." The poet ibn Doreid, in his well known kasida from the Yadthabia said: [M.S. Page 77.]

> "A thousand men are as one and one is as a thousand
>   "when affairs go wrong.
> "What God has hindered cannot be given and what God
>   "has given cannot be hindered.
> "And he whom God has exalted cannot be abased nor can
>   "he be exalted whom God has abased.
> "God is super-eminent above all and most noble of all.
> "He enfolds in His mercy whom He pleases and in His
>   "hands are all things.
> "And He doeth what He pleases."

May God increase the Sultan's majesty and the beauty of his renown and greatness; his goodness and his victoriousness; by the grace of our lord and master Muhammad upon whom be the blessing of God and peace, and by the grace of his companions, the chosen ones, who followed, and of those who followed them; and by the grace of Jibrail and Michail and Israfil and all the prophets and messengers of God. May the blessing of God and peace rest on them all Amen! Amen!! Amen!!!

Such is the account we have given of the character of our Sultan and his wars in the time when he was king. We have written it after there has passed of his reign twelve years.

We will shortly write an account of the wars that took place between him and the people of Kanem if God wills (exalted be He). God is the accomplisher of all aims and to Him all things return. [M.S. Page 78.]

NOTES.

M.S. Page 2.

Sheikh Masfarma Umr Ibn Othman.

This Sheikh who settled near Gumsa in Geidam district flourished about 1500 A.D. As is noted in the introduction, he wrote a considerable work on the history of Bornu which is stated still to exist though it has not hitherto come to light. Abridgments, however, of it existed, to which from time to time additions were made, and from which more or less accurate extracts or lists of Mais were also made which are found all over Bornu. Considerable variations occur between different versions, and none, which are at present in circulation, are as good as two copies of one abridgment called " The Diwan of the Sultans," which were obtained by Dr. Barth from the Shettima Makaramma about the year 1853.

One of these copies of the Diwan was sent to the German scholar Otto Blau and published by him at Leipsig. The other copy, Barth's own copy, is also now available and has here been translated, p. 84 *et seq.*

Its text is in parts rather corrupt and to do it justice full explanatory notes would be required. For the purposes of this book, however, I append a simple translation of the text, which may be compared with Otto Blau's text and translation and Barth's chronological synopsis of the reigns of the Mais (in Vol. ii of his travels, p. 633).

The meaning of the text for the most part is clear enough, though some of the names as written in the Arabic obviously need explanation or emendation.

In all cases, however, where I have materially departed from the manuscript reading, I have placed my reading or emendation in brackets.

Certain dates which are approximately accurate have been inserted in the margin, and a few footnotes added.

There also exists in the Kanuri language a song or rythmic chant giving the names of all the Magumi Mais. It was sung by the N'gijima, Babuma, and Zakkama at Court, and is called like other genealogical accounts of the Kanuri a " Girgam."*

This Girgam of the Magumi has, in years, through slips, mistakes and omissions in the repetition of a long list in which the same names occur many times, become confused and transposed in places, but at the same time it sheds a good deal of light on the Arabic " Diwan," and the reason why the order of the reigns has been lost is observable by study of it.

It is also observable that descriptions of earlier Mais are attached to later ones of the same name as nicknames. Several versions which differ somewhat *inter se* exist, the best on the whole

---

* *Vide* Mr. Patterson's Kanuri Songs. (Government Press, Lagos.)

being that published by the writer in the *African Society's Journal* some years ago.

The copy now owned by the Mufioma, however, as transcribed by Mr. J. R. Patterson, is much the same, and is therefore appended to the "Diwan," the Mais (so far as identification seems certain or in some cases probable) being placed in the order in which they occur not in the Girgam, but in the Diwan.

The order of the Mais, however, 1-17 and 53-66 is the same in both Diwan and Girgam.

Appended are also genealogical trees showing—

(a) Dunama Dabalemi (1221-1259), and the rival families of Idris Nigalemi and Daud Nigalemi.

(b) Ali Ghaji Dunamami (1472-1504), and the Mais descended from him down to the time of the sack of N'gazargamu by the Fulani, after which Bornu was ruled by the Kanembu Sheikh Muhammad al Amin and his descendants, though for some time a titular Mai was maintained by them for reasons of policy, as shown in the Girgam.

M.S. PAGE 2.

Idris ibn 'Ali ibn Ahmad ibn Othman ibn Idris.

This is the grandfather of Idris Alooma. He reigned from 1504 to 1526. In the year 1512 he sent an embassy to Tripoli.

His father 'Ali Ghaji Dunamami is generally called 'Ali Ghaji Zenamami following the usual rule that descent through the mother is recorded. He founded N'gazargamu about 1472, acquiring the site from the "So" who lived in the region.

He is said to have acquired as much land as a bullock's hide would cover, and to have cut the hide into thin strips to make it go as far as possible.

The name of the capital is correctly spelt—N'gazargamu or N'gasarkumu. The first part of the word N'gasar signifies that the previous inhabitants of the region were N'gasar or N'gizim. The latter part of the word—gamu or kumu—is the same as the first part of the name "Gwombe" and means either (i) chief or king or (ii) ancestral spirit.

Very little is known about Ahmad, generally called Dunama, the father of 'Ali but his date was about 1450 A.D. His name comes in the list of numerous itinerant Mais who lived towards the end of the civil war, between 1432-1472.

Dunama's father, however, Othman, called Biri, was regarded as the rightful Mai from about 1400 to 1432. Othman must, during that period, have led a wandering life without real authority over anything but his own following. His Kaigama or war chief Mohammad ibn Dallatu seceded from him and fighting took place between them.

Othman was the younger brother of Mai Umr who in 1398 finally left Kanem, and fled to Kagha.

The father of Umr and Othman (Biri) was Idris Nigalemi who was reigning in A.D. 1353 when the traveller ibn Battuta returned from his visit to Melle and Songhay by way of Tekidda

South-West of the present town of Agades. According to Barth's chronology Idris reigned from 1353 to 1376.

M.S. PAGE 2.

Saif ibn Dthi Yazan from the flower of the Kuraish, and the seed of Himyar.

This is probably in substance and fact incorrect, though it is possible or indeed probable that some Arab adventurer married into the Kiye (Kayi) Barbars, and so was a factor in the origin of the Magumi, or Saifawa as they are called.

With regard to this line of Mais (Sultans) from which Idris sprang, called in Bornu Saifawa, it may be premised that in documents contemporary in date to Idris, they bear the title Makidâbe " of Makida or Makada "—*i.e.*, the region of Northern Kordofan West of the cataract region of the Nile.

The tradition that they came originally from Yaman in Arabia is one common to other Muslim peoples of these regions an example being the origin ascribed to the mediæval rulers of the Dongola region by the Muslim historian Makrisi.

On the other hand the Kanuri speaking races of Kanem (Kanembu) who must necessarily represent a fairly early stratum of in part Hamitic stock, all believe that their origin was in Yam, this same region or a little to the North of it, on the West bank of the Nile, which was called by the name of Yam as far back as the days of the middle kingdom of Egypt. The ethnography therefore of the peoples of Kanem and Bornu is closely bound up with the past history of the Nile Valley, and country to the West of it, more particularly with the Jebel region of Northern Kordofan and the Wadi Malik region.

The earliest Mais were undoubtedly ' white ' not ' black ', *i.e.*, Barbars of some sort, who counted descent through their mothers. Their mothers were either Tebu or Barbar (Tuwareg). They could not well have been Arabs.

The problem therefore of the origin of the Bornu Kingdom and its Mais (kings) is in a measure the problem of the peoples known to the ancient world as Ethiopians, who, though often mentioned, were so far outside the pale of the civilised world, that scanty details concerning their culture and mode of life have come down to us, or at least scanty reliable details.

Among the Ethiopians known to the ancient world were the so-called ' White Ethiopians ' Leucaethiopes.

The Leucaethiopes have been invoked by various writers to account for the existence of the Fulani in West Africa, but there is very little evidence that the Fulani existed as a people in large numbers before about 1050 A.D. and even then, they were apparently a nomadic people who formed encampments in the neighbourhood of large indigenous towns in the Upper Niger and Senegal regions. Thus beyond vague impressions derived from map makers who thought that the Upper Nile region and what is now called the Bight of Benin were fairly close together, there is no strong evidence for placing Leucaethiopes in West Africa.

On the other hand the probability is that the differentiation of the Fulbe (Fulani) from other Barbars was due to racial fusion with the 300 Tyrian colonies which were planted in the Wadi Draa region during the first millennium B.C.

The spread of and multiplication of the Fulani as a negroid race was due to inter-marriage of the Fulbe with the indigenes of the Senegal region—Tacrur.

All natives of the West are at the present day known in the Eastern Sudan region by this name. On the other hand the regions to the North of the Senegal were populated by Barbar tribes who, as the Arab writers tell us, were from the time of the invasion of West Africa by Ocba and other Arab leaders, permeated by many heterogeneous elements.

We have very definite statements that the early rulers of Ghana or Ghanata in that region were white and were in close contact with the Almoravides, by whom they were influenced and to whom they were at times subject.

As regards the other or Eastern half of the Sudan, we have two important facts which are drawn from the Arab authorities.

The first is that the early rulers of Kanem, that is to say, the Saifawa dynasty of Bornu, were of the tribe of Zaghawa.

The second is that according to ibn Khaldun, these Zaghawa belonged to the second race of Sanhaja Barbars, who had multiplied in the vast plains between the Upper Nile region and the "rif" of Abyssinia. Ibn Khaldun states elsewhere that certain North African Barbars had joined the Zaghawa. There can be no question that if these authorities are correct about the genesis of the early kings of Kanem and the Zaghawa, races which were of white affinity were the ruling factors in the regions East and North-east of Lake Chad as far as the Nile down to about 1000 A.D.

The skin colour of the Kanem rulers is shown by many circumstances as, *e.g.*, the fact that it is specially stated of one of the early kings of Kanem that he was the first Sultan who was not white.

Again the Bornu court historians have endeavoured to arrange their line of Sultans on a patrilineal basis, though it is very evident that as regards the succession to the Sultanate matrilineal descent was the only thing that counted in the earliest times.

The Kanuri (that is to say, the inhabitants of the Kanem kingdom) in the 16th century called the Tuwareg Barbar, but they did not call the Tebu by that name. The peoples to the West of Bornu on the other hand called the Kanuri "Beriberi" which is merely a local variant of Barbar. It would appear that the reason why the Barbar, *i.e.*, white Barbar or Libyan, origin of the early kings of Kanem and Bornu, has not been recognised is that in later times Bornu became so permeated with Tebu influence, its language being related to that of the Tebu and Brabra of the Nile, that the real origin of its kings was obscured and, as is customary, their genesis was ascribed to an Arab of distinguished ancestry to wit, Saif ibn Dthi Yazan.

In fact, however, Leo Africanus does tell us the truth, for he states that the kings of Bornu were *lineal descendants of the Libyan tribe of Bardoa*.

This passage, so far as I have seen, has been misunderstood—for it is assumed that Bardoa means ' Tebu '—because the Tebu are now dominant in the areas where these Bardoa roamed.

On the contrary it appears that Bardoa is merely a variant of Barbar being composed of the root ' Bar ', the Kanuri ' ti ' or ' di ' which means ' land or land of ' and the plural suffix ' awa ' or 'oa ' " people ".

The key region in regard to this point is naturally the Kauwar oasis and Tibesti and Borku. There, tradition is unanimous that the Tebu were the indigenes and were the inhabitants of the Tibesti and Kauwar regions before they were conquered by the early kings of Kanem about 1200 A.D., *i.e.*, the Tebu under their commoner name of Gara (Guraan or Garawan) were the ' swift footed Aethiopians ' whom Herodutus called Garamantes, having a more or less civilised capital city in the North, Garama in Fezzan.

It was against these Tebu occupiers of the Kauwar oasis that we must assume the early Arab expedition from Fezzan was launched at a time when Jawan in the North of the oasis was the capital.

But just as the Tebu races called the capital city of Fezzan Gara-ma, *i.e.*, place of the ' Gara,' so also they called the modern capital of the Kauwar oasis Bul-ma, *i.e.*, the place of the ' Bul '. *i.e.*, whites, people of the Barbar (Beriberi) stock (the rulers of Kanem) who conquered the indigenous Tebu and developed the natron trade of the oasis.

From the time of the Kanem (Kanuri) conquest of Tibesti and Kauwar therefore, *i.e.*, from about 1200 A.D. the ruling people of the Kauwar oasis were Kanuri (Zaghawa), and it is these who are the Bardoa of the Arab authors, the Libyan tribe of Bardoa, from whom the rulers of Kanem were descended.

Another argument lies in the apparent fact that the Zaghawa and Beli (Bidevat) speak the same language, and appear to be differentiated sections of what was once a people of Tuwareg not Tebu affinity. The Beli (under the name of El Beliun) are spoken of by Edrisi as being Jacobite Christians and raiding Assuan, and are by Dozy equated to Blemmyes.

Another rather significant piece of tradition is that the early rulers of Mandara, South-east of Lake Chad, combined.

(*a*) A Tuwareg connection of some sort;

(*b*) A Kanuri genesis;

(*c*) Some tradition of having been Christians at one time.

It seems rather relevant to this subject to note that the name of the country where the Beli (Bidevat) live and have lived so far as can be judged for at least 1,000 years, *viz.*, Annadi is composed of the two Kanuri and Tebu words Ana (or Ama) = people and di (or ti) = earth or land, also that among the Beli and Zaghawa, Bar plural Barri, is a word for ' man ', corresponding to the Kanuri Kam (singular of Ana or Ama).

Now the Kanuri word for Tuwareg in general is Kindin, a

word which seems connected with forms like Makinta (chief of a village), Ama-Kitan (Tuwareg of the Southern Sahara) as well as with the place name Anadi (Ennedi).

The inference from these various forms, seems to be that the word Anag, used in Kordofan to denote an autochthonous Barbar race of giants, is merely the Kanuri-Teda word ' An ' with the Tuwareg termination -ek or -ag. The An-ag would naturally live in An-di (Annadi), and be called by the Kanuri of Kanem and Wadai Kan-di-in = Kindin.

A variant name for the Anag is Abn Gonaam. Here also in the case of the Kwararafa or Kwona, who were in origin cognate to the ancient rulers of Kanem, they claim as a point of departure in migration from the Nile Valley the " Jebel Kwon " said to be in Kordofan.

In Kanem during the 16th century near the town of Sulu there was a tribe apparently different to the other Kanem tribes called by the chronicler Kananiyin, who were probably of Tuwareg affinity—*i.e.*, imghad or servile Tuwareg.

Tura on the other hand is the common Tebu and Kanuri term which is applied to the white races of the North (*e.g.*, of Fezzan) whence the common designation of a ' white man ' in Hausa, Ba-ture plural Turawa.

With regard to the root of the word Barbar, *i.e.*, Bar = man, as it is a common noun and a third personal pronoun in the Zaghawa and Beli languages, its use in place names in those regions explains itself. We may compare such names as Barku (both Wadai and a region West of the Niger), the Baranes of ibn Khaldun (*i.e.*, Southern Barbars who came from the East) Barabish (tribe North-west of the Niger), probably Barti (Berti), and the Kel Buram who are said to have invaded Mandara at an early date.

It would seem in fact, if conjecture on such a vast subject is permissible at all, that the earlier Hamitic stratum throughout the Sahara and upper part of the Eastern half of the Sudan, were the Tebu, Teda, or Gara (Gurá'an) peoples who called themselves An (Am) or Ana (Ama) whence the ancient Egyptian term for them.

Then at a later date, following ibn Khaldun's belief, a large group of peoples whose word for man, men, was Bar, Barri, etc., grew to large proportions in the country between Tibesti and Abyssinia, included among these being the Blemmyes and other Aethiopians known to the ancient world.

The final stage would seem to have been the blending of these " Bar " races with North African or Libyan races, so that the " Bar " languages came to predominate over almost the whole of North Africa, leaving the pre-existing Gara stocks the Tebu, Garamantes and ancient Nobatae, and later the Kanuri, like islands in the middle of an encircling Barbar flood.

Certain scholars have, I believe, made comparisons between—
    (*a*) The Kanuri language and the Brabra dialects of the Nile;
    (*b*) The Brabra dialects and ancient Sumerian.

If the inference one would naturally draw from these comparisons is correct, it would seem to suggest that these races are the Kash (Cushites) of the Egyptian monuments and that the early white races' in Kordofan Wadai Darfur, and Bornu were ibn Khaldun's "second race of Sanhaja," who spread North of the Tibesti Massif, till, as ibn Khaldun says, they occupied the whole Sahara, and incidentally provided ruling dynasties for most of the Northern part of the Sudan—from Kanem to Ghana in the West.

With regard to the latter (Ghana) it is interesting to note that its first or 'white dynasty' which ruled before the Hejira of the Prophet, was called Kayamagha. As the second element in this word is a Barbar word for 'great' we have the somewhat curious coincidence that whereas the Ghana rulers were Kaya, the tribal mothers' stock of the early Kanem dynasty which began soon after the Hejira, was also Kayi or Kiyi.

A connection between the two is definitely suggested by traditions, having of course the usual Muslim garb, which are recorded by the Timbuctu Arab historians, to the effect that an invasion under a member of the army of the Ummayad Caliph Umr ibn Abd ul Aziz, founded both the Kingdom of Bornu (Kanem) and the Kayamagha dynasty of Ghana. (*See* the Tarikh el Fettach).

Further than this the subjects of the 'white dynasty' of Ghana were the Wan-gara or Wa-kore, *i.e.*, just as the Tebu (Gara) were the subjects of the Kayi (Zaghawa) of Kanem, so were the Wan-gara (*i.e.*, Gara people) subjects of the Kaya-magha of Ghana.

This analogy between East and West is carried still further by a fact noted by M. Israel Hamet in his work on Mauretania, *viz.*: the servile clans of the Sanhaja Barbars were and still are called 'Anbat', *i.e.*, the Anbat of the Sanhaja.

It seems not unreasonable to suggest the equation of these Western Anbat to the Nile Nobatae, who coming originally from the Western oases of Egypt were settled in the cataract region of the Nile by the Romans, with the help of whom they crushed and dispersed the Blemmyes from the Nile Valley about 400-500 A.D., and became the basic element in the Christian Dongola Kingdom of which the language—now represented by the Brabra dialects—is in structure very similar to the Tebu and Kanuri languages.

Surveying the whole field, the conclusion to which one inclines is that the ancient rivalry between the Nobatae and Blemmyes was only the first phase or manifestation of a conflict which has gone on ever since between the earlier Kushite (Gara) races of the Sahara and Sudan like the Tebu, and the later Barbar races who like the Blemmyes rose to a dominating position in the Eastern Sudan and Sahara between about 500 B.C. and 500 A.D., the latter being partly, if we may believe the Arab traditions, migrants across the Straits of Bab el Mandeb from Asia though doubtless having in a large measure a Libyan, *i.e.*, Tehenu, admixture.

Had these peoples been of the ordinary type met with in North Africa or Libya, the sight of them at a 'triumph' would hardly have astonished the Romans in the way which, we learn from Volpiscus, it did.

But when about 500 A.D. the Blemmyes were crushed in the Nile Valley a great people like them can hardly have vanished without trace. We hear of them in the time of the patriarch Nestorius as seizing oases in the Western desert which Imoshagh (Tuwareg nobles) were to occupy, while ibn Khaldun assigns to the Sanhaja and Kitama in Fezzan an Arabian origin that did not admit of doubt, an origin similar to that ascribed by the Greek and Roman writers to Blemmus and other mythical heroes of Meroe who stood for a " chivalry " not unlike that of the modern Tuwareg, which had " fought against Bacchus " in Asia.

The sequence of events and such history of Northern Africa as has come down to us seems to indicate that the Blemmyes revenged their defeat at the hands of the Nobatac in the East by becoming ibn Khaldun's second race of Sanhaja, and overrunning the West from Kanem to Ghana, making tributary to themselves as servile tribes (imghad) the same Nobatac (Gara) races who had, with Roman help, driven them from the Nile Valley.

M.S. PAGE 3.

Muhammad ibn Mani was a contemporary of the early Muslim Mais of Kanem. In certain mahrams (grants of privilege) which are still preserved, he is stated to have read the whole Kurá'an with Mai Ume Jilmi (1086-1097) the first Muslim Mai of Kanem, having previously read portions of it with Ume's predecessors.

Mani's descendants were hereditary chief Imams at N'jimi and afterwards at N'gazargamu.

It is very probable that the name Mani is a variant of the Meroitic form of the god Ammon's name, *viz.*: Amani, for the name is also used to denote the mythical ancestor of certain Kanembu tribes or clans.

As Barth points out (Travels, vol. i. p. 60) Ammon (Amun) was the chief deity of the pagan Barbars, the word meaning probably " Founder or Supporter ".

Among the Tuwareg the chief of a clan is Amano-kel, *i.e.*, the 'supporter' of the clan (kel), while their word for God is Amanay (Barth).

M.S. PAGE 4.

Sultan Haj Idris ibn 'Ali ibn Idris.

Legends concerning the youth and upbringing of Idris Alooma are numerous and it is difficult to distinguish fact from fiction.

It would appear, however, that his father 'Ali ibn Idris Katagarmabe died when he was an infant and that he was brought up by the Queen Mother or Magira. Aisa Kili N'girmaramma, a remarkable woman, who built for him a brick palace, standing as a ruin to this day on a beautiful stretch of the River Yo at Gambaru, so that he should not be exposed to the evil influence of the capital N'gazargamu.

It is stated, whether correctly or not, that Idris Alooma's mother was a daughter of a Mai of the Bulala, and that on the death of his father 'Ali, she had the greatest difficulty in preserving his life during the reign of Dunama son of Muhammad, who succeeded, and of his son Abd ul Lahi ibn Dunama

The majority of the lists of kings now extant attribute to Idris a reign of fifty-five years. This as Barth showed must be wrong. He reigned in fact from 1571 to 1603, thirty-two years, and it seems probable that the residue of the period of fifty-five years is roughly the period from the death of his father 'Ali, to his accession, on the death of Abd ul Lahi ibn Dunama, *i.e.*, his father 'Ali ibn Idris Katagarmabe died about 1548, his reign not being so short as the chronological table given by Barth states.

Idris met his death at the hands of a pagan archer said to have hidden himself in a tree in the neighbourhood of the present capital of Bornu—Maiduguri—a region then inhabited by Gamargu and Mabani. He was buried, according to tradition, in the middle of the Alo Lake, whence his name Alo-oma.

An effulgence at night, is still said to be visible, owing to the sanctity of his remains in the middle of the Lake, where his body lies.

The red brick palace of Shau Dorshid in Darfur is called to mind by the brick buildings of the old Bornu capital N'gazargamu, Gambaru on the Komadugu, and other places. These, however, only date from about 1500 A.D., and were probably built under direct Nubian or Egyptian influence.

M.S. PAGE 4.

Al Haj Daud ibn Nigale.

Daud and his brother Idris were the sons of Mai Ibrahim who was a son of Mai Dunama Dabalemi and is mentioned by Makrisi as reigning about 1300 A.D.

Confusion has occurred in Barth's list owing to Barth apparently mistaking the nickname Bîri which was used for Mais called Othman for Bura which is short for Ibrahim.

Ibrahim's nickname was Nigale whence his sons were called Idris Nigalemi and Daud Nigalemi.

Mai Dunama Dabalemi as we learn from the "Kanem War" uncovered a talisman (Muni or Mani) which his predecessors had kept covered up, and which was probably "Ammon" (Amani).

The result of this was, according to the Imam, that strife and civil war ensued. Though on Dunama's death he was succeeded by his son Abd ul Kadim (Kadai) who reigned twenty-nine years the latter was even after a long reign, murdered.

To him succeeded Bîri another son of Dunama Dabalemi. Biri was succeeded towards 1300 A.D. (*vide* Makrisi) by his son Al Haj Ibrahim. Ibrahim ruled till he too was murdered, and succeeded by Abdallah a son of his uncle Abd ul Kadim.

It is interesting to note that Ibrahim was drowned in the Komadugu Yobe near Geidam and buried at Diskam which has the explanatory title N'galaga-tin, *i.e.*, "in the country of the N'galaga." It seems therefore probable that the first Kanuri tribe which came in any numbers West of Lake Chad was the N'galaga and thus that this tribe were the founders of a settlement near N'gazargamu in the "So" country, a long time before the Mai Ali Ghaji finally settled there.

Now the variant and, in Kanem common name, of the N'galaga is N'galma N'diku. From the latter of these words comes the Bornu title of the chief who was in charge of the Fellata (Fulani) who were located in the West, *viz.*, N'dikuma (Digma).

It seems apparent that the original N'dikuma was the clan head of the N'diku (N'galaga), and thus that the name of the murderer of Abd ul Kadim (*see* Barth's Vol. ii, p. 638) should be N'dikuma Dunama not Andakama Dunama.

We may infer that the N'galaga were hostile to the Abd ul Kadim branch of Dunama Dabalemi's family and friendly to the Ibrahim (Biri) branch. Subsequently Ibrahim himself was murdered in this same N'galaga region not by the N'galaga but by the Yuroma, a palace official.

Though Abd Allah, son of Abd ul Kadim succeeded, it is evident that the N'galaga in revenge incited the " So " to resist the authority of the Kanem Mais. Abd Allah's sons were one after another killed by the " So " Tatala of whom we read in this history.

Subsequently the whole of the N'galaga region became subject to the N'gal-ti-ma, *i.e.*, Galadima of Bornu, who ranked at N'gazargamu next to the Mai.

When later on the line of Biri (Idris Nigalemi) was restored in the person of Ali Ghaji Dunamami (1472), the N'galagati region, as being most favourable to his family, was chosen for the capital N'gazargamu.

We see later in this narrative that other regions had espoused the cause of the rival family of Mai Daud Nigalemi, who from the time of the accession of Mai Umr, son of Idris, in 1394, had more or less allied themselves to the Bulala of Fittri.

M.S. PAGE 5.

The Kauwar Oasis.

In the age of Herodotus (500 B.C.) Southern Fezzan and the country to the South of it was occupied by people known as Garamantes. They were of two kinds (*a*) those who lived in the capital city Garama, who had evidently absorbed a good deal of Egyptian or Libyan culture and had horse-chariots; (*b*) the desert Garamantes called also Ethiopians who were nomads and spoke like ' bats.'

That these desert Garamantes were substantially the same people as the Tebu now called Garawan or Guraan is generally held to be certain. The name of their capital city, Garama, is the correct Teda-Kanuri form for the " place of the Gara."

In Roman times Garama was called Jerma. According to Pliny (N.H. 1.v.c. 5) the road to Garama was not open till the time of Vespasian, when the present route from Tripoli *via* Mizda and Gharian to Jerma (North-west of Murzuk) was first used and called the *iter præter caput saxi*.

From an inscription found by Barth it is further evident that in Marcus Aurelius' time Gharian was an outpost which, commanding this road, had come into existence as a military post in 232-235 A.D. or even before.

From the ruins of forts and castles and sepulchres which survive to-day as far South as Jerma, it is evident that the Romans were well established in Fezzan until the appearance of the Vandals under Gaiseric soon after 400 A.D.

To the Vandals succeeded Belisarius the Byzantine general. Under the Emperor Heraclius many Barbars became Christians. The ruins of a church of Byzantine architecture still remain near Mizda.

We may perhaps presume that till about the period of Vandal ascendancy the population of Fezzan had remained fairly homogeneously Gara (Tebu), but between 400-500 A.D. a great movement of races—Barbar races—set in from the Upper Nile Valley through the Western oases to Fezzan. These people were the Tuwareg—the Beranes of Ibn Khaldun. They formed in Fezzan the great confederation known as the Hauwara* (modern Hoggar) while further West they were called Sanhaja and further South and West Zaghawa.

It is stated by Duveyrier and doubtless the statement refers to these same Barbar tribes that between the time when the Vandals ceased to dominate Fezzan and the Arab domination which began in 666 A.D., a Bardoa dynasty—probably Christian—ruled at Jerma (Zeila).

This statement is doubtless well founded and it accounts both for the traces of Christianity found among the modern Hoggar and Ibn Khaldun's statement that whereas the Jerawa (Garawa) of the Aures mountains were of the Jewish faith, the other Barbars of North Africa were Christians.

The Jerawa (Garawa) belonged to the older sub-Libyan population—Gaetules—whereas the new Barbars who had followed the Christian Jacobite heresy from the time of Justinian and the Empress Theodora, were mainly Donatists, because that heresy represented antagonism to the established church of the Byzantine Emperors.

That the influence of these Bardoa chiefs of Jerma extended to the Kauwar oasis is evident and we probably find in Idrisi an echo of their rule in Kauwar in the place name Kasr Um Isa 'mother of Jesus,' a site which is still called Gasbi or Kasarwa.

In 666 Okba ibn Nafi' made his expedition into Cyrenaica and Fezzan, and penetrated as far South as the Kauwar oasis of which Jawan (mentioned in this history) was then the capital.

In 670 A.D. Okba with headquarters at Kairuwan became ruler of North Africa. He was succeeded five years later by Abu el Mahajar but in consequence of revolts Okba had to return in 679. At this time the sectary Abn Yezid in Tunis was in full revolt. Okba seems to have pursued a policy of making the leading Barbar chiefs renounce Christianity.

He was, however, in the end ambushed and killed by the Barbar leader Koseila who then assumed power in North Africa.

About 688 the Khalifa Abd ul Malik had to send as Governor

---

* In Bornu the Hauwara were called Hauwaza. Mai Arki in one Girgam is said to have died at "Zeila Hawazalan" in "Zeila among the Hoggar Tuwareg."

to Africa Hassan ibn Noman who was opposed by the valiant Barbar Queen Kahena. About the year 693 A.D. Kahena, after laying waste the whole country in a futile effort to save it, was slain.

Thus ended, at least in Fezzan, real Barbar independence—and it can hardly be doubtful that thousands of Barbars sought safety further South in the Sudan.

In Zeila from this time onwards there were Arab Governors or chiefs. It is observable from the writings of Ibn Haukal, Yakubi, and others that their prestige extended South as far as Kaukau on the Niger, and no doubt equally so in the direction of Kanem, of which the inhabitants so late as the time of El Bekri (1050 A.D.) are classed as pagan by Arab writers.

Towards 900 A.D. we have Yakubi's account of Zeila, showing that a large number of merchants from Khorasan and elsewhere had congregated in Fezzan to engage in the slave trade.

Complementary to this is an account given in the chronicle of the kings of Bornu (*vide* the manuscript Barth sent to the scholar O. Blau) to the effect that Mai Arki (whose probable date is soon after 1000 A.D.) " had many slaves, and settled 300 of them in Dirku (Kauwar) 300 in the oasis of Siggedim (Yat) to the North of Kauwar, and 300 at Zeila."

About the middle of the century 1000-1100 A.D. came the utter destruction of Fezzan by the hordes of the Beni Hilal and Soleim.

The fights between Abu Zeid el Hilali and the Tuwareg of Fezzan, called by the Arabs Illam(t) or Allam(t), are graphically described in the existing folk-lore of the Dikwa Iesiye Arabs who trace their descent to the Beni Hilal.

The result of the Hilalian invasion of Fezzan was that chaos ensued in Southern Fezzan and the Tebu country, and it was not until the time of Dunama Dabalemi (1221-1259) that the Mai of Kanem's power extended up to Kauwar and Zeila. This is stated as a fact by the Arab writer Abul Fida and confirmed by the Bornu chroniclers. Zeila continued to be subject to Kanem till about 1400 or so.

Traces of this period still exist in such Bornu titles as Jerma (*i.e.*, the ruler of Jerma), Zeilama (ruler of Zeila), Amarma (ruler of the Beni Aamer who ruled in Tripoli from 1323-1399). During the Kanem civil war the Gara (Tebu) became not only independent of the Kanem dynasty of Saifawa, but came down and allied themselves with various Kanembu clans and the Bulala.

No doubt Idris placed chiefs of his own choosing at Jawan (the old capital of the oasis) at the stronghold of Ashenumma (Ahanama), at Bulma, and at Aghram, where the big salt deposits are, to the West.

M.S. PAGE 6.

Barâk, *i.e.*, the Wadi Barâk situated on the present Borku-Kanem road between N'galaka (Faya) and Mao.

There is a tradition that a town now called Barara North of Mao was destroyed by a Mai returning from Mecca.

It seems evident that the 'musketeers' were brought from Egypt through the Kufra region and Borku to Bornu.

M.S. PAGE 7.

Kuburi-Kayi.—The original Beni Kayi, the Kayi (or Kai) Bulala, and the present Koiyam or Kileti are virtually the same people in origin.

The Kayi women intermarried with Arabs formed the royal clan of Magumi.

The Kayi men intermarried with the N'gizim population of Fittri formed the Bulala or Ikilalan.

The descendants of the original Kayi who have maintained a nomad life and are still—save that most of their camels were destroyed by Rabeh—camel owners, are now called Koiyam or Kileti.

They are classed as Tura, *i.e.*, whites. The Kuburi on the other hand are said to originate in Fukara (Muslim fakirs) who came to Kanem from the East.

There always has been antipathy between the Kuburi and Kayi and still is.

Muhammad al Amin the Fakir who in 1810 drove the Fulani out of Bornu and founded the present dynasty of Shehus belonged to the Amsawa clan of the Kuburi.

M.S. PAGE 7.

Gamargu, Marghi, Kopchi, Mishiga, N'garasa.

This is the region extending from the present district called Nguma-ti along the Yedseram valley down to Mubi and Uba.

The N'guma (whence N'gumati) are regarded as of "So" origin, though they have become so mixed with Kanuri that they are now a Kanuri tribe.

The Village Head of N'guru Begua in the East of the present district of Marghi bears the title Mai N'garasa.

The reason doubtless that these peoples concerned themselves with the rivalry between the two branches of the Magumi was that when Mai Umr Idrisimi in 1398 finally fled from Kanem he settled in the Kâga region between Uje (Alo Lake) and Gujba, now part of Marghi district.

The two most important local chiefs in the present Marghi district are Mai N'garasa and the Kâgama.

The pre-N'guma and pre-Gamargu inhabitants of these regions were called M'bum. They are said now to inhabit regions on the Upper Benue River.

M.S. PAGE 7.

N'gizim.

There are various forms of this name which though they are distinguished seem to denote the same people—N'gijim, N'gujam, N'gazar, N'kazzar, N'gisam.

By some they are designated Fellata or Badu (Badawin) whence the name for a portion of them the Bade (Bedde). They seem both East and West of Lake Chad to have been fishermen and hunters and to have, even in early days, had domestic animals, mainly sheep and cattle.

Some of them seem to have inhabited the Fittri region before the coming of the Barbar Kayi, for one Ali N'gisammi is said to have been the uncle of the Bulala.

At the date of the narrative, the most Easterly settlement of Binawa N'gizim in what is now British Bornu was probably the site of the present station called Maiduguri though its real name is Mafoni or Mabani—Mabani being equivalent to Binawa.

In all probability the Alo River which flows to the North of the Government Station was the boundary between the Mabani (Binawa) and the Yedi inhabitants of N'gumati (the Ala region) to the North of the river.

M.S. PAGE 12.

Geterama, i.e., the chief of the town of N'getera in the North of the present district of Gubio. Damasak is on the Komadugu Yobe further North.

Kardi, i.e., heathen.

M.S. PAGE 18.

Zimbam—now called Jimbam, in Borsari district. N'gazar is in the Danani unit in the same district.

M.S. PAGE 21.

Kirki, i.e., Kirik Nagu on the Yobe to which Idris Nigalemi is said to have fled even before his successor Daud was killed by the Bulala.

Dagambi—in Geidam district, in N'galagati unit on the Komadugu Gana.

Tura—is a loose term meaning people of Northern origin usually light in colour.

M.S. PAGE 25.

Noble Shah—See introduction.

M.S. PAGE 28.

Stockade of Sultan 'Ali ibn Ahmad—i.e., N'gazargamu which was at first only a stockade.

M.S. PAGE 29.

Chief of Yamta—the Barbur (Pabir) chief who had settled in the region of the modern town of Biu. In the legends of the Mais of Biu the name Yamtarawalla is given him. These chiefs claim descent from the Saifawa of Kanem (i.e., Zaghawa). According to the Gamargu traditions the Babur did not come to the Biu region from N'gazargamu but through Fis in Musgu and the Marwa region.

At some periods of Kwararafa ascendancy in the Gongola region and at Bepi (Birnin Kwararafa), the Mais of Biu paid tribute to Shani who passed it on to Bepi or Kundi the Jukun capitals.

The Mai of Biu wears a pigtail like the Jukun "Aku" (king) and in other respect his customs and rites conform to those of the Jukun kings.

M.S. PAGE 30.

Tawati—The manuscript reads Tawati but as the Tatala were obviously somewhere in the Dikwa region and Idris was marching from Birni the correct reading must be Tuwati, *i.e.*, the region called Tuwan or N'jituwa behind Dikwa in Mandara.

Kaza—one of the old " So " towns, is about fourteen miles East of Dikwa. Amsaka is South-east of Kaza, not very far from Kala Balge.

As Amsaka is in the midst of a plain of dead flat black cotton soil which would be entirely inundated during the rains and well into the dry season, it is possible to fix the date of the fall of Amsaka, from the data given, with some certainty, *i.e.*, 4th December, 1575.

M.S. PAGE 37.

Mandara.

From investigations made by Mr. J. R. Patterson, it would appear that the population of Mandara, *i.e.*, Kerawa, and the country stretching back to Uje and Alo Lake on the West, and Kaza on the East, was Gamargu, the proper name of that tribe being Amolgwa (whence Mulgwi).

The king of Mandara, however (and the ruling caste) were a different race called Wandala, who according to tradition were Barbars, of much the same origin as the royal dynasty of Kanem, *i.e.*, Zaghawa.

According to the Gamargu, they were driven from the regions East of their present habitat by Babur (Barbar) who advanced from the region of Fis (near Musgu) Balda and Waraga Dubuwa.

It may be noted that according to tradition the inhabitants of Amsaka spoke the Mandara language (*i.e.*, Gamargu), and that the present Marghi and Burra languages belong to this group, Mâsa languages.

Amsaka, Maidibi (a site near Gumsa in Dikwa) and Mandara Garu (the region where the king of Yamta lived) are reputed all to have been ruled by the same kind of people.

The sum total of the inferences to be drawn from this information is that the Babur and the Dajo, were much the same, *i.e.*, branches of the Zaghawa, like the Kanuri Mais, and that they occupied this region from Musgu to Biu during the 12th and 13th centuries.

The Mandara region is by the present ruling race themselves called Kagh(u) Wandala or Kaghu-n-Dala, *i.e.*, the " mountainous region of the South," and they called themselves Ara (*Agha*) Wandala, while they called the Kanuri Mathake (Amasek).

Barth states (Travels, Vol. iii, p. 178) that " The Musgu or
" Masa Museku, as they are called in Baghermi, and the Kotoko,
" or Magari, the people of Logone, the Ur Wandala, with the
" Gamargu and the Batta (Marghi) and M'bana—are a division of
" the great nation of the Mâsa, while among the Kotoko, Ngala
" and Klesem seem to be most nearly related to the Musgu."

It is difficult to account for factors which are common to this Mâsa group, though they now differ widely *inter se*, except on the basis of a common invading factor from the North-east, *i.e.*, from Wadai and Borku. The names Masa and Musgu irresistibly suggest Masigh and Amasek as also the Mandara tradition of the Kindin Kel Burum who settled in the region before the founding of N'gazargamu.

In this same region and to the South of it there grew up between 1000 A.D. and 1300 A.D. the great confederation of tribes known as Kwararafa. Presumably sometime between 1100 and 1350 A.D. they founded the towns in the Gongola region, Biyri, Kalam and Kundi, which were afterwards the seat of their power, whence, later on, they made expeditions and sacked such towns as Kano and Katsina, while in the 17th century they besieged the Mai of Bornu himself in his capital N'gazargamu.

Between 1349 and 1385, during the reign of Sarki Yaji of Kano, the Wangarawa (*i.e.*, Songhays), so we read in the Kano chronicle, came to Kano, and established Islam as the State religion there. Yaji ruled from Biyri to Pindika so the chronicle states.

At the end of his reign Yaji is said to have attacked the Kwararafa in the Biyri region who fled up the rock of Attagara.

Again, during the reign of Muhamman Zaki of Kano (1582-1618):—

"The Sarkin Kwararafa came to attack Kano; the people "of Kano left the city and went to Daura, with the result "that the Kwararafa ate up the whole country and Kano "became weak."

It is perhaps not without significance in connection with the Kindin Kel Burum of Mandara, that the earliest settlement of the invading peoples who founded the Hausa kingdoms was Burum ta Gabbas near Hadeijia. There can be very little doubt that these invaders were Barbar of some sort and that they passed through parts of the Sahara, possibly the Bulma region which was later regarded as part of Bornu. They were not influenced by the Tebu races but on the contrary caused the language we call Hausa to be a Barbar language akin to Tamashek.

Assuming the correctness of existing data as to penetration of the Mandara and Gongola regions by Zaghawa and Dajo under one name or another from the 12th century onwards or perhaps before that century, it is difficult to see how the Kwararafa who followed the same line of migration at about the same epoch, can have been a migration of peoples of a very dissimilar type to the Zaghawa especially in view of the fact that all Kwararafa tradition asserts that they were a branch of the Barbar (Beriberi) of Bornu, *i.e.* Kanem.

The most notable feature about the Kwararafa organisation was that they were a caste, a hieratic caste, who dominated groups of other tribes much as their descendants the Jukun of Wukari did formerly in the Benue region or again the Aro of Aro Chuku in the Ibo country did in more recent years.

In general all tribes associated with the governing caste were called Kwararafa, the ruling element itself being called by the Kanuri, "Kwana" or "Kwona" by the Hausas Jukun, and by the Wukari Jukun themselves, " Apa ", while at Aro Chuku this same hieratic caste were called " Inokun ".

We find in the Kanuri language parallel to the Tuwareg forms Imoshagh or Imajaren which mean ' free " or ' nobles ', the forms Kokana ' a noble ' plural Kokanawa, as also the form Nokena ' council of nobles '.

The Hausa form corresponding to the Tuwareg ' Imoshagh ' is the common noun ' Miji ' a man, plural ' Mazza.' This is equivalent to the Kanuri ' mag ' in such forms as ' magira ' ' queen mother ', ' magumi ' (the royal clan) and ' magge ' the Bulala word for the " ruling " or " noble " house.

It would seem therefore that the words ' kwon ', ' kwana ' were cognate to the Kanuri forms ' Nokena ', ' Kokana ', *i.e.*, belonged to a pre-Zaghawa language of Kanem or Wadai, and are in fact connected with the Kanuri, ' kam ' or ' koa ' (man) just as the Tamashek Masigh is connected with the Hausa ' miji ' (man) and ' mazza '.

We also have probably a variant of this form ' kwon ' in such names as Gwom-be, N'gasar-komu and the words ' gwom ' ' kom ' for king which occur in a number of existing dialects in the Gongola region. The ruler of Wukari (Jukun) is called the " Aku(n)."

The other form ' Apa ' which is used to denote this same caste South of the Benue as, *e.g.*, in the language spoken now by the Jukun, is perhaps a variant of -aba or -ab which in the Eastern Hamitic language means ' men ' or ' people '—the equivalent of the Western -awa.

It is noticeable that the old Birnin Kwararafa in the Benue region is by the Apa (Jukun) called Bêpi, while the god or deified ancestor of various tribes of Kwararafa connection in Southern Bauchi, *e.g.*, at Gwana and Pindika, is called Bappi.

The inference from these facts, if indeed it is permissible to draw one very tentatively, is that the Kwararafa spoke a language of the Hausa-Tamashek group while still living to the East of Lake Chad, and that later nomenclature given them by the Teda-Kanuri speaking peoples who constituted the Kanem Kingdom accounts for the name Kwona, and such names as Kun-di, Biy-ri, Gwom-be, etc., which are Kanuri forms.

In origin, however, it would seem that the Kwona or Kwararafa were probably akin to the Zaghawa and Kayi, so that possibly Kwon and Kundi and Kindin (" Tuwareg " in Kanuri) are from the same root, and are not unrelated to Kinaniyin a tribal name which Imam Ahmad, in his later work on the Kanem war, mentions as having been that of a people who at one time dominated part of Kanem.

There certainly exists a certain amount of evidence, particularly in the isolated village of Attagara in the Mandara hills, to support the tradition of the Kwararafa (Jukon) themselves that, leaving the Nile Valley about 600 A.D. they migrated by slow stages from the Jebel Kwon (Kordofan), through Magge (Fittri) and Balda and Fis in the Mandara region to the Gongola Valley. Both they and the Bolewa of Fika and Gombe were probably branches of the Pabir (Barbur) who according to Gamargu tradition came from the East and drove them out of the Mandara hills.

The predecessors of these Babur or Kwararafa tribes in the Marghi region and perhaps in Mandara also, would seem according to tradition to have been races called M'bum.

Concerning them Mr. Patterson has collected two interesting accounts from manuscripts in the possession of Marghi chiefs, in one of which it is stated that " the chiefs in Maifoni (Maiduguri) ruled over the people who went to Bumwa in the land of the Emir of Rai (Rê Buba) ".*

In the other " the Sultan of N'gazargamu sent a messenger to the land (Marghi) the inhabitants of which were the M'bum.

M.S. PAGE 37.
Hawk, i.e., the three Sultans of Kerawa (Mandara), Mulgwi (Marghi), and Yamta (Biu).
Bumi Data. The first word should probably be M'bumi, i.e., a town formerly belonging to the M'bum who had lived in these regions.

Dat was the name by which many tribes in the Fali (Bauchi) region knew the Jukun (Kwararafa) and such may be its meaning here.

M.S. PAGE 38.
Kano Stockades. These stockades lay in the country intervening between Kazra (*i.e.*, Kazaure) and Majia which lies to the South-west of the town of Hadeijia.

According to the Kano chronicle the son of Bauwo who became the first king of Daura was named Kazura. It is also there stated that the invaders (Bagoda) who afterwards founded Kano settled first in the district of Sheme, *i.e.*, the district between Damerghu (in Kano Emirate) and Kazaure.

Buram-ta-Galbas, previously founded by Bayajidda, lay to the North of Hadeijia on the road to Gure.

In the time of Sarki Yakubu of Kano (1452-1463), a son of the chief of Mashinna. North-west of N'guru, who was probably a Barbar or half Barbar of some sort, came in to Kano and was made Sarkin Gaia (East of Kano), while his brothers were made chiefs of Hadeijia, Dal and Gaiam (in Zaria) respectively.

The Dulu here mentioned is Duru in the same region—whence the name of the river Duduru.

It is recorded in the Kano chronicle that between 1509-1565, *i.e.*, the period covered by the reigns of Mai Idris Katagarmabe and his brother Muhammad, certain Muslim Sheikhs named Karashi, Magumi, and Kuli came to Kano from Bornu. Magumi was made Kadi at Kano and appears to have dispensed justice at the gate of the palace.

It was through the region of these stockades (the present Berde district of Kano Emirate) that Mai Muhammad would pass to his famous battle with Tomo (Kanta) of Kebbi when the latter was slain in his camp at the rock of Dugul near Dan Ashita in the Ingawa district of Katsina Emirate.

---

* Now in the Cameroons, South of the Benue.

About the year 1565 the Sarki of Kano by name Yakufu, was deposed after reigning four months, by his Wazir Guli in favour of his son Dauda Abasama. The latter again was deposed after reigning one month, and Abubakr Kado, a son of the famous Muhammad Rimfa made Sarki 1565-1573.

It appears that Yakufu retired to a district now called Yakufawa in Katsina South-west of Ingawa, and that his sons the Sarkis of Kazura (Kazaure), Majia, Gilima, Taura, and Gwunka and his daughter who ruled at Buduru, were also deposed.

All these places are in this same district, as also Karmashe (near Ringim) to which Dauda Abasama, son of Yakufu retired. The line was restored to the throne in 1573 in the person of Muhamma Shashere another son of Yakufu.

Since Yakufu and his son Muhamma Shashere were evidently very well disposed to the Bornu people, the Alkali of Kano being actually a Magumi, it seems evident that it was the chiefs of this region put in by Abubakr Kado who caused Idris to make war upon Kano.

It is also evident that what is now a southern part of Kano Emirate was at this time under the control of the Kwararafa, *i.e.*, the districts called Fali.

In the Kano chronicle the son of the Sarkin Mashinna mentioned above, who was made Sarkin Gaia is rather loosely called Agalfatia, the meaning being that he, Sarkin Gaia and ergo the Sarkin Machinna were of the people called Agalfatia.

The Agalfatia are Bugaje, *i.e.*, ' servile Barbars,' and are so called because in vending, as they do, quack remedies, love philtres etc., in Hausaland, they pronounce the " Fatiha."

Their real name is thus Agar or Agal, which may be compared with the forms Targi-aga (Dagara) and Agal-awa, a people who inhabited a town called Agar or Agal North of Geidam, and founded colonies of merchants at Shibdawn in Katsina, Gerko in Kano, and other places.

It is clear that these Agar or Agal (in part servile Tuwareg) were the people who founded the reputation of the Hausa as an itinerant trader. They are the ' Beriberi ' who in Yakubu's time (1452-1463) came to Hausaland in large numbers and traded to the West, becoming in many cases the people who are now called Kambari or Gambari.

M.S. PAGE 40.

Stockade of Dalla. Though the word ' Shokiya ' should mean " a stockade " it is probable that its meaning must not be pressed to exclude a town with a mud-wall. In the case of Dalla (Kano) a wall had existed since the time of Gijimasu (1095-1134) which was extended by Mohamman Rinfa (1463-1499) and by Mohamma na Zaki (1618-1623). As the term for this type of town (Birni) came from the name of the capital of Bornu (Birni N'gazargamu) the Bornu historian was probably unwilling to admit the existence of another Birni and so called other towns Shokiyas (stockades) though the stockade was built of mud. In the case of Amsaka also, no doubt the town was a ' birni '—*i.e.*, had a mud (sun-dried brick) wall.

According to Kano tradition the first invaders who came to Kano—apart from the aboriginal negroes on Dalla hill—were called 'Abajiawa'. They settled with their herds near Gaia East of Kano.

The Kano chronicle probably alludes to this, where it is stated that "the Sarkis of Gano, Dab, and Debbi (near Gaia) came to Hausaland before Bagoda," the founder of Kano.

The resemblance of the name Abaji-awa to the name given by the Arabs to the Eastern Hamites—Beja or Boja—is noticeable.

Bagoda, before he came to Kano, was for some time settled at Sheme, between Kazaure and Damarghu (Kano) circa. 1000 A.D.

It is also stated in the Kano chronicle that Abd ul Lahi Burja (1438-1452) was the first Sarki of Kano to pay 'gaisua', *i.e.*, tribute to the Mai of Bornu. It is generally stated that Ali Ghaji Dunamami who founded N'gazargamu about 1472 had for some years previously been established at Yamia to the North of Mashinna and South of Munyo. It is possible that it was he, as a young man, who made an expedition to Asben from Yamia and made Kano pay tribute to him, as recorded in the Kano chronicle.

On the other hand the date of Abdullahi Burja 1438-1452 seems a little too early, and the Mai in question may have been one of Ali Ghaji's immediate predecessors who ruled after Mai Othman Kalinwama or Kalinwa fled to Kano during the time of Sarki Dauda (1432-1438).

The Sarkin Kano Muhamman Kisoki, ruled from 1509-1568. Of him the Kano chronicle relates that—

> "The Sarkin Bornu sent to him and said 'What do you
> " 'mean by making war'? Kisoki replied: 'I do
> " 'not know, but the cause of war is the ordinance of
> " 'Allah'. The Sarkin Bornu came to attack
> "Kano, but could not take the town and returned
> "home."

A minstrel of Kano called Dunki apparently celebrated the Mai of Bornu's defeat by a song which began "Kisoki physic of Bornu and the Shiratawa" (*i.e.*, people of Shira, who were in origin Dagara (Dankir)).

The Mai in question was probably Idris Alooma's predecessor—Abd Allah son of Dunama N'gumaramma.

M.S. PAGE 41-46.

Tuwareg—Ahir—Gamaram—Kutushi.

By this date (1570) the Asben Oasis had been occupied by the Tuwareg Iteseyen, who nominated the chief of the country, the Kel Giris and the Kel Lowi. The town of Agades had already been built, the oasis and surrounding country being known as Ahir or Air.

According to the records of the people of Agades their first king had been nominated or, at any rate, approved by Stambul, *i.e.*, the Turks, about 1400 A.D. or shortly after.

The older name of the oasis was, however, Asben or probably more correctly, its variant Absen, for the name of its central range of hills, written Baghsen is, probably the same name as Absen, the root being identical with that found in Habash, Ahbasan, Abasenoi, etc., and in fact being the same word as is now written and pronounced **Hausa**.

It may be that a Roman expedition under one Julius Maternus which penetrated the Sahara in the first century of the Christian era and got as far as a place called Agisymba did, as some writers think, reach the Absen oasis. If so Agisym-ba is a very ordinary metathesis for Ba-ghsen or as it is pronounced by the Hausas Bagasam.

At any rate the Absen region was the earliest known home of tribes speaking the present Hausa language, or an early form of it which was later much modified by, if it was not entirely recast by contact with the Tamashek Barbar tongues of the Sahara.

Either contemporaneously with or at some period before the occupation of Kano by Barbars (Bagoda) toward 1000 A.D. a clan or tribe to which the name Gobir or Gobar (Bargu) is given occupied the Absen region, and were masters of the oasis, till, as the Asben chronicles say, " when their rule grew weak, they were " conquered by the Beriberi."

Now this conquest must have taken place before the date of Ibn Battuta, since in his day Guber (as he writes the name) lay to the South of Tekidda (three days South-west of Agades).

As the conquest by Beriberi does not mean the conquest by the modern Tuwareg tribes of the region, which occurred later, it must mean conquest by the Barbars who made Tin-Shaman (a village to the West of the road from Auderas to Agades, and about twenty miles North of the latter) their capital. Barth (Vol. i p. 336) states that it had been the capital at least since the 16th century.

But since the prefix ' Tin ' means ' possessor of ' and since as early as the time of Idrisi (1150 A.D.), Shama or Sama was a place name which denoted settlements of the Zaghawa Barbars, there is little doubt that the Barbars who conquered the Gobirawa were the Amakitan cousins of the Zaghawa who founded the Bornu-Kanem dynasty. The Amakitan are now in fact a subject tribe in the Absen Kingdom which is ruled by the Kel Giris and Kelowi.

Other Barbars who were in the Absen region in the time of Ibn Battuta, called by him Takakari, were sections of the Ulimmiden even then beginning to migrate from the North to the Upper Niger region.

Now between the Absen or Ahir country and the Bornu capital N'gazargamu, there intervened two regions.

   (1) The region of Munyo and Gure—a hill region—called by the Kanuri Kutushi.
   (2) The region of Damarghu called by the Kanuri Gamaram.

The former was really part of the Bornu Kingdom the latter was not, but inhabited mainly by tribes which though not classed as noble Tuwareg (imoshagh) were so called servile clans—imghad (sing: amghi), of the Barbars.

The place names Damagram, Damarghu, and Maradi are all derivatives of this Tuwareg root meaning ' servile '—as well as the Kanuri term for Damarghu, *i.e.*, Gamaram—the root being m(ar), m(ir), k(ar), k(ir), (g)ar, (g)ir—whence also the names of the old capitals of this region Mir and Mirria, the Mirriin of Yakubi, who were exported to Fezzan as slaves, and the very old site of Marmar in Hadeijia.

These servile tribes from a very early period must have occupied the country intervening between the healthy central Sahara, where the Imoshagh preferred to live, and the Sudan proper which was the home of the negro populations.

In this account of Mai Idris Alooma's war with the Barbar (Tuwareg) we have a typical example of these servile peoples in the 'Dankir' which means the tribes located in the Damarghu and Munyo regions called by the Hausas Dagara or Diggera and sometimes Dagirawa.

In the legend of the foundation of the Hausa Kingdom the Barbar hero Bayajidda, having escaped from the king of Bornu, married a woman of the Diggera or Dagara, who was left behind at Biram-ta-Gabbas (Garun Gabbas) and gave birth to Biram there.

The children of this woman would naturally be "servile" from a Barbar point of view, from the desert rule that it is the status of the woman that counts.

Barth (Vol. ii, pp. 71 and 72) states that "Biram is univers-
"ally represented as the oldest seat of the Hausa people and also
"the mother of the Sarkis of the six other Hausa states belonged
"to the Dagara or Diggera tribe." He remarks that many Diggera lived in Daura, so that possibly a reconciliation between this version and the more current one nowadays that all the Hausa kings were descended from a Queen of Daura, lies in the probability that Daura and Dagara are the same word.

Bayajidda in that case will be merely a legendary personage like Saif ibn Dthi Yazan in the legends of Bornu, and the people who are represented by Bayajidda and Bagoda will be the Dagara tribes which were no doubt servile to the Imoshagh of the Amakitan, whence the Hausa Sarkis are said to be servile (imghad) to the kings of Bornu (the Beriberi).

In fact it would appear that the root (m)ar, (g)ar, (k)ar, though its original signification was merely 'people' (*cf.*, the Hausa "iri"—seed) came to mean in the Barbar languages or among the Barbars in general—'servile peoples.' That is its use among the Kanuri in the termination agha (ara), and the division of Idris Alooma's army into ahel dark (Barbar nobles) and ahel gara (in general the Tebu), seems to point to a similar connotation of the word among the Kanuri in early times.

It is noticeable that in the Kano chronicle Bogoda (*i.e.*, the old Numidian name Bogud), before he came to Sheme (Kazaure) and Garazawa (near Kumchi) in Kano, is said to have lived at three places which are not in Hausaland and must have been to the North of it, called Dirani, Barka and Talutawa.

Dirani seems to be the Tamashek word for mountains "Deren;" Barka may mean the North generally from Barka, *i.e.*, Cyrenaica, and Talutawa may be an allusion to Ibn Khaldun's theory of the descent of the Tuwareg from the Philistines.

In any case the intention of the writer is clearly to convey that the invasion came from the desert zone, and from the track of the invasion it is probable that it consisted of Dagara who at that time occupied the regions of Damarghu (Gamaram) and Kutushi as far South, at any rate, as Mashinna a place name which, with Kashinna (Katsina in the West), is due to these Barbar tribes and not to the later Kanuri Kingdom at N'gazargamu.

According to local legends Damagram (Mirria) was founded by a Dagara hunter called Kutukum, and even now the facial markings are practically similar in the case of:—

    (1) The Dagara.
    (2) The Daura Hausas.
    (3) The Kutumbawa of Kano—*i.e.*, the descendants of Bogoda (the Hausa kings of Kano).
    (4) The Auyokawa of Buram-ta-Galbas and Hadeijia.
    (5) The Shirrawa of Shira further South and the Teshinnawa near Katagum.

The first two of these have two plain strokes on each cheek, the three latter have these two strokes shaded (lemu).

The inhabitants of Damagram called Mashinna indifferently Kashinna and Mashinna, and further South (near Katagum) lies Teshinna founded by the same Dagara, and at least two other Dauras now in Bornu.

In view of these facts it will hardly be surprising that—

    (1) The Kano chronicle states that the Sarkis of Rano, Dab, and Debbi, East of Kano, came to Kano before Bagoda.
    (2) In the reign of Yakubu (1452-1463) sons of the Sarkin Mashinna were given posts under the king of Kano, as Sarkis of Hadeijia, Dab, and Gaia respectively.

It was just at this period that Ali Ghaji Zeinami was, from Yamia North of Mashinna, carving out for himself a kingdom in the West. No doubt the sons of the Sarkin Mashinna (Dagara) came to Kano because their father had been deposed or killed by Ali; from whose time Mashinna was incorporated into the Kingdom of Bornu.

It may be added that Zaghawa in Kordofan told Mr. H. A. MacMichael that they counted among their stock two peoples called Kobir and Daura.* That is practically the same thing as saying that the Dagara were 'servile peoples' of the Amakitan who were a branch of the Zaghawa.

An old manuscript of some authority which is in the possession of the Alkali (Kadi) of Sabonbirni, Sokoto Province, relates that the Goburawa, people of Gobur or Kubar (Gubar), were in origin a tribe who fought against the Muslims, we may perhaps suppose, somewhere in the Sahara. It continues: " The Goburawa arose " thence and left Gobur and came to the salt mines of Balma " (Bulma) where King Baba Turmi died. Then the Goburawa " choose Bachiri as king of Gobur at Balma. He never went to

---

* MacMichael " Tribes of Northern Kordofan."

" war, but lived there till his time was finished and he died. Then
" the Goburawa again assembled and chose Dalla as king of Gobur
" at the salt mines of Balma—the Asbenawa used to come to buy
" salt at Balma . . . . Then the king of Gobur . . . . entered the
" land of Asben."

According to the local chronology this was about 700 A.D. Assuming the substantial correctness of this narrative the obvious inference is that the Ku(Gu) -bar were a Barbar tribe who inhabited Bar-ku (Borgu) about 700 A.D.

The order of the two monosyllables which make up the name is immaterial. Ku or gu is the equivalent of -kwa, -owa, or -wa = people.

The Hausa legend that their kings, except Gobur which was free, were slaves of the Beriberi (Barbars) thus means that (a) the original chiefs of Gobur in Absen (Asben) were imoshagh, i.e., nobles descended from Barbar women; while (b) the kings of Daura (Dagara) stock who ruled the other Hausa States were servile in origin, i.e., imghad to the Barbar Amakitan (Makida) or Zaghawa.

M.S. PAGE 41.

Fellata—Fellata are first mentioned, as having come from Melle in the West to Bornu, in the time of Mai Biri, son of Dunama Dabalemi, circa 1288-1306.

In the Kano chronicle Fulani are spoken of as having first come to Kano in the time of Sarki Yakubu 1452-1463, bringing Arabic books with them, and as having passed on to Bornu. At the same period caravans began coming to Katsina from Gwanja (*i.e.*, Salaga on the Gold Coast), and Beriberi (Bornu people) came to Kano in large numbers.

From about this period 1400-1500 must have dated the influx of nomad Fellata from the West through Damagram into Bornu, where they settled mainly in the region N'guru-Damaturu.

Thence they passed in the 17th century down the Gongola Valley to Yola and Muri, where they are represented by the present ruling families of Yola and Muri.

In the 18th century they gradually sapped the power of the Kwararafa first at their old capital Bepi near Wukari, and then from their centre at Walamma on the Gongola they extinguished the Kwararafa power in Biyri, Kalam and Kundi in Gombe on the Upper Gongola.

The Tuwareg, no doubt began plundering the Fellata in Damagram and followed them up into Bornu.

Fulani (Fellata) were numerous in Kano in the time of Kutumbi (1623-1648), who collected the Jangali tax from the Fulani clans of Jafunawa, Baawa, Dindi Maji, and Danneji, so that no doubt the Fellata Idris sought to protect, were fairly numerous in Western Bornu.

M.S. PAGE 41.

Targi-aga, i.e., the " Dagara " called in Kanuri " Dankir."

The suffix aga or agha is pronounced " ara " in the North. It means ' servile ' as in the word Kaga or Kagha which meant the 'subject peoples' to the South of Bornu, the Kaigama or war chief of Bornu being really the Kaghama or 'master of the Kagha.'

The Dankir or Dagara were the servile tribes of the Targi (Tuwareg nobles or imoshagh).

The peoples called here Targi-aga, *i.e.*, servile races of the Tuwareg, are by the Hausas called Bugaji (sing: Buzu)—and further West they are called Bella.

The slaves of the Tuwareg on the other hand are called Takili or Takir (Dagir).

There is another class of people in these regions which extends as far West as Sokoto. In that region they are called Tozer or Tozamawa while further East they are called Tazar (hence the place name Tassawa, *i.e.*, Tazarawa).

The Tozer or Tazar are the people who originally worked the salt called Mangal to the North of Mashinna. They appear to have originated from mixed marriages between Barbars, and the indigenous tribes of the region.

Later, when they began to spread West to Katsina, their chief was a Bornu Zanua*, who was based on Mashinna.

During the time when the Katsina Kingdom was powerful, *i.e.*, from about 1450 onwards till 1750 or so, these Tazar spread greatly and became the chief agents in the trade to Gwanja (Gold Coast).

As they settled down and intermarried with the Katsinawa and other Hausa peoples they acquired the name of Kam-bari, *i.e.*, persons of partly Beriberi (Kanuri) descent.

Trade to the West was so entirely in their hands that Kambari (Gambari) in the West came to mean "Hausa."

M.S. PAGE 41.

Kileti—As has been noted the Kileti and Koiyam are identical. Barth (Vol. iv, p. 19) points out that the Kiye (pronounced generally Kayi in Bornu) comprise the Koiyam, the Magumi, and the Farfere clan who are under a Fugu.

He goes on to state that according to his informants the Jatku or Jetku were of the same stock as the Kileti.

Now obviously the Jatku are in origin inhabitants of the oasis of Jat or Yat North of Kauwar.

Similarly the present head of the Koiyam the Siggidrima (pronounced now Sugundirema) derives his title from the oasis of Siggidin(m).

It would seem then that during the period 1200-1400 when Bornu controlled the whole route to Tripoli, colonies of the Kiye (Kayi) being camel-men were planted at Yat and Siggidin(m).

The name, however, now pronounced Kileti is written by Imam Ahmad—Kilwati—and it appears not improbable that this, seemingly the older pronunciation, is an apocopated form of Kel Luwati, *i.e.*, Lewata (Libyans).

The form Koiyam is of course for Kwiy-am or Kiye-am. The statement in one Bornu manuscript that the original home of the

---

* *i.e.*, title—there was also a Zanua at Wukari in the Benue.

Kiye (Kayi) was at a place called Kabila on the Abeshe-Dongola desert road, and that the tribe were defeated there by Mai Abd ul Lahi Bikur about the period 1177-1193 (before they came to Fittri) has been materially confirmed by the re-discovery of an oasis called Ain el Kiye, hitherto unvisited by any European, in that region*

There is no reason against, and many reasons in favour of the Kiye being Lewata—Libyan Barbars—while the Barbar tribe Kitama again, who came into Fezzan with the Sanhaja and Hauwara and are by Ibn Khaldun given a partly Yamanite origin— may well be another group of these same Kiye (Amakitan).

The traveller Barth (Vol. iv, p. 4) writes " The Tawarek or " Kindin, as they are called in Bornu, claim a greater interest, " the Tuwarek or Barbars having originally formed an integral " part of the settled population of Bornu."

Makrisi (apud Hamakar Spec. Catalog p. 206), who wrote about 1400, also states that the ruling races of Kanem " are " descended from the Barbars " and that their king was " a " Bedawin in habit."

In a present day record it is stated that before the Kanuri Mais came to Kanem their kinsmen, the Amakitan or Kindin, ruled in the desert, and again that the Kayi ruled in the desert before the Magumi were established in Kanem.

There can be no doubt that the Beni Kiye (Kayi) the Amakitan and the Kindin (modern name for Tuwareg) are substantially the same—*i.e.*, Barbars not Tebu.

The ceremony, still practised under the Shehus, of installing a Sultan by raising him on a shield (dark), and the Bornu council of twelve chiefs (nokena), as well as the position of the Queen Mother (Magira) corresponding to the Meroitic Candace (Ki(n) ta-ki), are also very material evidence that the early Bornu Kingdom was Barbar not Tebu nor yet Arab.

M.S. PAGE 46.
Kasimwa—*i.e.*, Kiri Kasimwa in the North of the present Geidam district.

M.S. PAGE 49.
Gumsu—this is the title of the chief wife of a Mai of Bornu. Evidently Adwa considered himself a Kanuri.
Kerawa—South-east of Dikwa at the Northern end of the Mandara hills. To the East lies Mora the present capital of Mandara.

There are at Kerawa a number of tombs of the Wandala (Mais of Mandara).

M.S. PAGE 51.
Mugulum—now called Mugrum North of Potiskum.
Daura—*i.e.*, hilly country between Potiskum and Gujba. The Fellata were no doubt living mainly near Damaturu.

M.S. PAGE 52.
Binawa—*i.e.*, Mabani who extended from about the Borsari region West of Birni to Katagum.

* Newbold Sudan Notes and Records Vol. VII, p 34.

Mai Abd ul Lahi ibn Dunama—the immediate predecessor of Idris—according to Barth he reigned from 1564-1570.

M.S. PAGE 53.

The River—The river here means the Komadugu Gana which rising in Fali (Bauchi) flows past Misau and Mugulum (Mugrum) on to Zimbam (Jimbam) and then past Geidam to join the Komadugu Yobe North-east of Birni.

The Binawa were of course astride the road from Birni to Fali.

M.S. PAGE 54.

God made safe the road—the road was and is approximately the road which passes through the following places—North-east to South-west—Gasgamu, Bultua, Zigaji, Geidam, Jimbam (Zimbam) Dapchi, Bedde Gana, Jaba, Mugrum (Mugulum) Gamajam (N'gamazan) Gujam (Bana), Fika, water of Jiria, Komi, Kalam (old capital of Kwararafa) on the Gongola in Fali. The road follows the Komadugu Gana from Geidam to Gujam, which is probably the Gujambana of the narrative.

In all this region many ruins of old towns exist together with numerous boabab trees which were apparently planted by the N'gizim in their towns.

Mawa—on the road between Mugrum (Mugulum) and Gorgoran (Bade) near and North of Nosseri, an old town of the Leriwa.

M.S. PAGE 55.

Kaburawa—near Dapchi.

Marguba—in the present Kaga district between Maiduguri and Gujba.

Disi—not far from the present district headquarters of Fune.

Fika—the capital of the Mai of the Bolewa who were Kwararafa in origin. As no fighting is mentioned they were no doubt feudatory to Bornu at this time, the stream called Jinjina (now called Jiria) being the boundary between them and the Kwararafa of Kalam on the Upper Gongola.

Sade—lies between Potiskum and Darazzo in Bauchi.

M.S. PAGE 62.

Gugai-Katagum—This was the region occupied by the Teshinnawa or inhabitants of Teshinna, who:
   (a) are in race nearly related to the Dagara;
   (b) spoke a language (now no longer spoken) closely related to that of the N'gizim and Bade (Bedde).

The inference seems to be that the N'gizim were not unrelated to the desert races such as the Dagara, an inference which is supported:—
   (a) by the fact that the Kanuri regarded them as Badu (herdsmen);
   (b) that the N'gisam of Fittri intermarried with the Keyi (Bulala) and that there exist N'kazzar in Borku.

M.S. PAGE 64.

Kotoko—who now live in the region between Dikwa and Fort Lamy.

Notes.

They are the same people as the Tatala who at this time fled into Lake Chad and were in consequence called Buduma or ' reed people '. They were also called Yedi.

Magiburum—or Maki Burun in Magumeri district in the village area of Bornu Yessu.

Maba—i.e., Mafa in the West of Uje district, now bush.

M.S. PAGE 65.

Mara—probably on the Lebait river somewhere in the region of N'gala and N'difu (N'dibu). Mafati the Kotoko capital is rather further East.

M.S. PAGE 68.

Sabi—N'gala—Mongonu—Sabi must have been not far from Dikwa. N'gala and Mongonu are on the South-west shore of Lake Chad, the former being a very old ' So ' town.

M.S. PAGE 69.

Makari—The Makari or Magari and Kotoko are the same people. They are unusually tall in stature, whence the stories of the ' So ' giants in the Bornu legends.

Kusuri—is on the Shari river opposite Fort Lamy.

Mandara—i.e., Kerawa.

M.S. PAGE 70.

N'gazar—i.e., N'gazar Jajiri East of Jimbam (Zimbam) in Danani unit (Borsari district).

DIWAN OF THE SULTANS OF BORNU.

In the name of God the Merciful, the Compassionate. May the blessing of God rest upon the noble Prophet.

This is the Diwan of the Sultans of Bornu.

The first of them was the Sultan Saif ibn Dthi Yazan, the son of the king of Bagdad. His mother was a woman of Mecca. He was of the Beni Sakasi or Kasaki or **Maghzumi**. He was Saif ibn Dthi Yazan, ibn As Sah, ibn Luwai, ibn Al Haj, ibn Bukr, ibn Abi ul Haj, ibn Jami, ibn Jimala, ibn Hud, ibn Amir, ibn Wardı, ibn Halima, ibn Ismail, ibn Ibrahim, ibn Akhu **Azar**, ibn **Tajur**, ibn Sherukh, ibn Arku, ibn Amir, ibn Salih, ibn Arghu Arfakhshad Muhammad ibn Sam, ibn Nuh, ibn Salih Abir, ibn Musulim, ibn Khanukh, ibn Zaid, ibn Mabrak, ibn Fata Muttawashkhan, ibn Shitu, ibn Adam, upon whom be blessing and peace.

1. *The Sultan Saif* was king of the four corners of the earth in the age in which he lived. When the time of his death drew near he died in the land of Sima (*i.e.*, N'jimi). His reign was twenty years.

2. *The Sultan Ibrahim ibn Saif.*—His mother was Ayesha the daughter of Karama (Garama). He reigned sixteen years.

3. *The Sultan Dugu ibn Ibrahim.*—His mother was Afaluwa (Afanuwa), a daughter of the nobles.* Her tribe was the tribe of Kayi (Keyi). Thus was he also. He died in the land of Yari Arbasha. He lived 250 years.

4. *The Sultan Fune.*—His mother was Fukashi. He reigned fifty years.

5. *(The Sultan Arsu).*

6. *The Sultan Katuri ibn Arsu.*—He died in the land of Kuluwan (near Dagana) after reigning 250 years or some say 300 years.

Circa 1000 A.D.
7. *The Sultan Ayuma ibn Katuri, ibn Arsu.*—His mother was Tumayu, daughter of Mek Samia (Samina or **Shebina**). She was of the tribe of N'gal-aga of the Habash (*i.e.*, Tajowin or Kuka). He died in the land of Tatanuri (either Tatanuri near Dagana or Mons Tantano, *i.e.*, the Hoggar country), in the desert. He reigned twenty years.

Circa 1020 A.D.
8. *The Sultan Bulu ibn Ayuma.*—His mother was Ganjaya a daughter of the Zigana (Amazigh or Imoshagh). She was of the tribe of the Beni Keyi (Kayi) of the " ahel dirk."† He died in the land of Mangi (Maki) Jibidam (Zabatam). He reigned sixteen years.

---

* *Nobles.*—The Arabic word is ' sarâr '—which is the equivalent of the Tuwareg Imajaren or Imoshagh.

† The Dirki or Dirkiin were the Beni Kayi or Barbar nobles of the Dir (Dar) or " Barbar encampment," corresponding to the Tuwareg Imoshagh.

Diwan of the Sultans of Bornu. 85

9. *The Sultan Arku ibn Bulu.*—His mother was Azasanna a daughter of the San Anna (Tebu) of the tribe of Tumagari of the "*ahel gara*" (Garawan or Guraan). He was considering one day the great number of slaves he had. So he settled the slaves to the number of 300 in the land of Dirku (Kauwar), and settled another 300 in the land of Zeila (Garama or Jerma in Fezzan). He died at Zeila and reigned forty-four years. **Circa 1035 A.D.**

10. *The Sultan Shu ibn Arkaman (Ergamenes)* was then made Khalifa. Thus he was. His mother was Tagasu daughter of Gayu, of the tribe of Tumagari. He was very handsome, the handsomest man of his day. There once entered to him a girl —a daughter of the royal house—and seduced him by her wiles. They saw her wearing seven gowns by reason of her blandishments. Therefore daughters of the royal house are prohibited from visiting the Sultan. **Circa 1075 A.D.**

He died in the land Ghanata (Ghana) *Agaman (Tagaman), having reigned four years.

11. *The Sultan Abd ul Jalil ibn Shu.*—His mother was a daughter of Bikoru, of the clan of the Amarma (*i.e.*, of the Kauwar Oasis). He died in the land of the Gamaram (*i.e.*, Damarghu). He reigned four years. **Circa 1080 A.D.**

12. *The Sultan Ume ibn Abd ul Jalil.*—His mother was Teigaram† a woman of the Gamaram of the tribe of Keyi (Kayi). He died in the land of Masr (*i.e.*, Egypt). He reigned twelve years. **Circa 1086-1097.**

13. *The Sultan Dunama ibn Hume.*—His mother was Kinta a daughter of the clan Buram of the tribe of Tubu (Tebu). His horses numbered 100,000—his soldiers were 120,000, not counting mercenaries. None of the Beni Ume enjoyed greater prestige than he. **Circa 1098-1150.**

Among his noble acts were pilgrimages to the sacred house

---

* The manuscript reading transliterated by Barth—Ganta Kamna— must I think refer to a Ghana or Ghanata, for the word is spelt in the same way as 'Ghanata' in the west, while the 'Kamna' (Gamna) is obviously some compound of the Barbar aga or agha, and may stand for Aghmat, Agaman, Agham, or Aughain or Tagama.

The place in question may possibly be the famous Ghanata, or Augham in the Timbuctu region, which were flourishing at that time, but it more probably means "country subject to a Ghana," since one 'Girgam' has ' Ahir Kutushi " as the burial place of Shu Arkimi.

† Teigaram is the feminine of Teigama or Tegoma (an old Bornu title) and means the owner of Teiga or Teigo. Tigaram is said still to be the title of the Gumsu (Queen) among the Zaghawa to the north of Abeshe (Wadai). As regards the Kanuri statement that Abdulahi ibn Bikoru defeated the Kayi at Kabila near a well called Kâbar on the Abeshe-Dongola road five days north of Mazrub, Mr. Newbold (Sudan Notes Vol. vii) writes: "The only possible site in this barren desert which can be identified with "it is Teigo waterhole. (Not to be confounded with Teiga plateau) Long: "25″ 30′, Lat: 17″ 30′. About 130 miles due north of Teigo lies ain el "Kiyeh: it is obvious that this remote oasis takes its name from the Kiyeh "or Kayi."

of God on two occasions. On his first pilgrimage he left in Masr (*i.e.*, Cairo) 300 slaves, and on his second a like number.

When he was on his way to a third pilgrimage, and took ship, the people of Masr said to themselves "if this king returns from Mecca to his country, he will take from us our land and country without doubt." So they took counsel to destroy him. They opened a sea-cock in his ship, so that the sea drowned him by the command of God. His followers saw him in his white garments floating on the sea, till he vanished from their eyes, lost by the command of God, most high, in the sea of the prophet Musa. May God pardon him. He reigned fifty-five years.

14. *The Sultan Biri ibn Dunama.*—His mother was Fasam (*i.e.*, Fatima) daughter of the nobles (Askan = Mazigh or Masganna) of the tribe of Kayi. He was weak in his conduct of the Government. When a certain thief was executed, his mother heard of the execution from him and said to her son the Sultan " How is it that you have killed the thief in view of the command of God, most high, ' cut off the hands of thieves, male and female '."

For this his mother put him in prison. He submitted and remained in prison for a whole year. When the Sultan wished to be present at an assembly of the Amirs, and sit in the Fanadir* they insisted that the people should leave the place of audience. When the people had left, the Sultan would come in and take his place. When he wished to rise a similar procedure was adopted. Hence this custom as between the Sultan and Amirs which exists to this day, and which also obtained in the kingdom of Sana'a.

Biri died at Gamtilo Jilarge. He reigned twenty-seven years.

Circa 1177-1193.

15. *The Sultan Abd ul Lahi son of Bikoru.*—His mother was Zeinab daughter of a Kadala of the tribe of Tubu (*i.e.*, Tebu). He who was called Bikoru and the prince Bitku, were both sons of Sultan Biri who lived at Kheir Karasua.

Gumsu (Queen) Fasam the daughter of the Sakarama (*i.e.*, Sultan Biri's mother) took charge of the two boys and gave them 200 camels. She gave Bikoru 100 camels called ' Bikoru ', and gave Bitku a like number of camels called after his name.

Abd ul Lahi died at the town of Fifisi. May God have mercy on him. He reigned seventeen years.

16. *The Sultan Salma.*—His mother was Hauwa daughter of Abd ul Rahman. Her tribe was Dibbiri (*i.e.*, Tebu). The reason he was called by this name was that he was very black in colour. No Barbar of Sultan Saif's line was born black till Sultan Salma. They were all red like the Arabs.

His Muslim name was Abd ul Jalil, but by reason of his colour he was called Salma. Such was his appearance in life. He died at Fajaska (Fifisi) N'gizriwan. He reigned eighteen years.

---

* *i.e.*, a sort of 'cage' in which the Mai sat. See the illustration in Denham and Clapperton's travels.

17. *The Sultan Dunama ibn Salma.*—His mother was Dabale daughter of Bitku. She was of the tribe or house of the Magaram (i.e., official sister of the Mai). Thus he was. He passed to and fro in the land, and was very quarrelsome. He was the first to cut open a thing called Mune—the nature of which no one save God, most high, knows.

In his time there occurred civil war through the greed of his children and in his time also the princes went apart into different regions. There was no discord before this time.

His horses were 41,000 and he reigned forty years.

Circa 1221-1259.

18. *The Sultan Kadai.*—He and his mother were of the house of Matala. His mother was a daughter of Yunis of the house of the Magaram. When his end drew near he died at Lere N'gamutu. He was murdered by a man called N'dikuma Dunama. He reigned nineteen years.

19. *The Sultan Biri ibn Dunama.*—His mother was Zeinab daughter of the Lagamama*. During his reign there came to him two Sheikhs of the Fellata from their country Malle. When his end came he died at Sima. He reigned twenty years.

20. *The Sultan Ibrahim ibn Biri.*—His mother was Kagudi a woman of the Sakardawan. Her tribe was Kinkina. He was the first Mai who executed his son. When his end came, a man called Yuroma Muhammad ibn Kadai threw him into the river. It is said that he was thrown in at the town of Zui-Zui. They took his body out at the town of Diskam.

Circa 1300 A.D

The Sultan Abd ul Lahi ibn Kadai (whose mother was Fatima) said to the people of the district who took the body out of the river " come and I will ennoble you." When they came he executed them all turning his face away from the nakedness of the Sultan.

Ibrahim's tomb is in the town of Diskam. He reigned twenty years.

21. *The Sultan Abd ul Lahi, ibn Kadai.*—His mother was Fatima. He was the most just man of his age. There was civil war between him and his companion the Bagharimma Gayu, son of the ruler of Katsinna (Matsinna).

When his end came he received news of four thieves sons of one mother. The Sultan sent for them to his presence and ordered the Lawan to cut their throats. The Lawan did so.

Therefore the mother invoked the Almighty as witness to the theft and prayed that the seed of the Sultan might be cut off. God hearkened to her prayers. The Sultan died at Shima (N'jimi). He reigned twenty years.

22. *The Sultan Salma ibn Abd ul Lahi.*—His mother was named Kime (red). Thus he was. When his end came he died at the town of N'difu in a war with the So, after reigning four years.

23. *The Sultan Kore As—Saghir ibn Abd ul Lahi.*—Thus he

---

* Lagam was in the region of Logone.

was. When his end came he died at the town of N'geliwa at war with the So. He reigned one year.

24. *The Sultan Kore Al-Kabir.*—Thus was he. When his end came he died at N'geliwa at war with the So. He reigned one year.

25. *The Sultan Muhammad ibn Abd ul Lahi.*—His mother was Kagala daughter of the *Wârama. Thus was he. When his end came he died at Nânigam Tagará'an at war with the So. He reigned one year.

Circa 1353-1376. 26. *The Sultan Idris ibn Ibrahim.*—His mother was Hafsa daughter of Nâsa(m)u. Thus he was. When his end came, he died at Sima, or some say Damasek, but the former is the more reliable account. He reigned twenty-five years.

Circa 1377-1386. 27. *The Sultan Daud ibn Ibrahim.*—His mother was Fatima daughter of Nâsa(m)u. In his time occurred war between royal princes and the Sultan. Thus was he. He was the first Mai who fought the Bulala. When his end came, he died at Malfe (in Fittri) killed by king Abd ul Jalil of the seed of Ume (Jilmi). He reigned ten years.

28. *The Sultan Othman of the family of Daud.*—Thus he was. When his end came he died in the land of Shima (N'jimi) at war with the Bulala. He reigned four years.

29. *The Sultan Othman ibn Idris.*—His mother was Famafa (Aisa). Thus he was. When his end came he died in the land of Shima (N'jimi) at war with the Bulala. He reigned two years.

30. *The Sultan Abu Bakr Layatu ibn Daud.*—Thus he was. When his end came he died at Sefiari N'gazriwan at war with the Bulala. He reigned nine months.

Circa 1394-1398. 31. *The Sultan Umr ibn Idris.*—Thus he was. When his end came, the war with the Bulala became heavy upon him. The Ulema assembled. The Sultan said to them: "Give us your counsel." The Ulema said: "Leave this place; our day here is done." Then the Sultan Umr ibn Idris brought out his armies and treasures, and all his people to the Kagha (*i.e.*, South) nor has any Sultan returned to dwell in Kanem till this day, nor will they ever. When Mai Umr's end came he died at Damagia. He reigned five years.

32. *The King Said.*—Thus he was. He died at Dagage at war with the Bulala. He reigned one year.

33. *The Sultan Kade Afanu ibn Idris.*—Thus he was. He died in Guluru (or Gaduru) at war with the Bulala. He reigned one year.

Circa 1400-1432. 34. *The Sultan Biri (Othman) ibn Idris.*—Thus he was. In his time there was a civil war with the Kaigama Muhammad ibn Dallatu. When his end came he died in the land of the

---

* *i.e.*, ruler of Wâra—the old capital of Wadai.

Kanantu. (*i.e.*, Kwana or Kwararafa). He reigned thirty-three years.

35. *The Sultan Othman Kalinwama ibn Daud.*—Thus he was. Kaigama Nigale ibn Ibrahim and Yarima Kadai Kafagu deposed him. He died in the land of the Afanu (*i.e.*, Hausas) at Kano. He reigned nine months.

36. *The Sultan Dunama ibn Umr.*—Thus he was. When his end came he died at Nanigam. His horses were to him as mothers. He reigned two years.

37. *The Sultan Abd ul Lahi ibn Umr.*—Thus he was. In his time there was a civil war with Kaigama Abd ul Lahi and the N'galma (*i.e.*, N'galma Diku or N'galaga).
Kaigama Abd ul Lahi deposed the Sultan, and placed on the throne Sultan Ibrahim ibn Othman. Then he restored the Sultan after the death of Ibrahim ibn Othman. When Abd ul Lahi's end came he died at Malfe. He reigned eight years.

38. *The Sultan Ibrahim ibn Othman.*—Thus he was. He held no court and was exclusive, nor did he cover the land with his majesty but listened to hearsay. When his end came he died at Zantam (North of Gambaru).
The son of his maternal uncle, Kadai ibn Kalinwama, murdered him. He reigned eight years.

39. *The Sultan Kadai ibn Othman.*—Thus he was. In his time civil war broke out between him and Sultan Dunama ibn Biri. When his end came he died at Damaza (Damasek). He reigned one year. **Circa 1450 A.D.**

40. *The Sultan Dunama ibn Biri (Othman).*—Thus he was. When his end came he died at (Dagara) Kowwa.* He reigned four years. **Circa 1451-1455.**

41. *The Sultan Muhammad ibn Matala.*—Thus he was. When his end came he died at the town of Damaza (Damasek). He reigned five months.

42. *The Sultan Amar(ma)*—son of Ayesha daughter of Sultan Othman. Thus he was. When his end came he died at Yarimiya (Yamia). He reigned one year.

43. *The Sultan Muhammad ibn Kadai.*—Thus he was. He was a cruel and tyrannical Sultan. When his end came he died at Magi Jibidam (Maki Zabatam) of the Kirbure (Kel Bure).

---

* The place of his death is transliterated by Barth as Agha-kuwah. This means the Agha (ara) of Kowwa (rocky place). We know that the family were about this time at Yamia in the region called Kutushi Kowwa (*i.e.*, the rocky Kutushi). I think the first part of the name may mean Dagara (Dankir), *i.e.*, Kutushi Kowwa the region of the " Dagara "—the first 'd' after " balad " being omitted.
It will be noted that this is almost exactly the time at which the Kano chronicle states that the King of Bornu made an expedition to Asben.
It is possible that the Damasek where the royal family lived at times during this period is Damasek (generally now pronounced **Gammashak**) near Munivo but I incline to think that it is the well-known **Damasek N.E.** of Geidam in the Yobe river.

44. *The Sultan Ghaji ibn Amar(ma).*—Thus he was. When his end came he died at Mangul Gamaram. The Kanemma (*i.e.*, Bulala Mai of Kanem) killed him with his sword. He reigned five years.

45. *The Sultan Othman ibn Kadai.*—Thus he was. There was war between him and Sultan Ali (Ghaji) ibn Dunama. He reigned five years.*

46. *The Sultan Umr ibn Abd ul Lahi.*—Thus he was. His chiefs did not assemble in council. He ate all the goods of Sultan Muhammad ibn Muhammad. Therefore Sultan Muhammad ibn Muhammad followed him as Sultan and no one rebelled against him. When his end came he died at Gamtilo Jilarge. He reigned one year.

47. *The Sultan Muhammad ibn Muhammad.*—Thus he was. He was a powerful and warlike monarch. He died in the country of the Barbars (*i.e.*, Sahara). He reigned five years.

Circa 1472-1504.
48. *The Sultan 'Ali ibn Dunama.*—Thus he was. He fought against Sultan Othman ibn Kadai and killed him and after that made Said (Umr) Sultan. After that the fighting among the Beni Sef subsided. When his end came, he died at N'gazargamu. He reigned thirty-three years.

Circa 1504-1526.
49. *The Sultan Idris ibn Ayesha.*—Thus he was. In his time the war with the Bulala cooled. He drove them back and took from them the land of Shima (N'jimi). He reigned twenty-three years.

Circa 1526-1545.
50. *The Sultan Muhammad ibn Idris.*—Thus he was. In his time was the war with Kadai ibn Lefia. He captured Kadai. Sultan Muhammad ibn Idris ibn Ali Dunamami ibn Zeinab spent nineteen years of his life at the town of Lade. He was a warrior and fortunate. His power extended to the boundary of Kabara. He died at N'gazargamu. He reigned nineteen years.

Circa 1545-1546.
51. *The Sultan 'Ali ibn Zeinab.*—Thus he was. He was just. He did not leave the path of justice till the day of his death. He died at Zantam. He reigned one year.

Circa 1546-1563.
52. *The Sultan Dunama Muhammad.*—In his time there was war between him and Abd ul Jalil ibn Gumsu. In his time also was the great famine called Bu Ihagana. He died at N'gazargamu and reigned nineteen years.

Circa 1564-1570.
53. *The Sultan Abd ul Lahi ibn Dunama.*—In his time was the famine called Sima Azadu which lasted seven years. He died at Kitala.

Circa 1571-1604.
54. *The Sultan Idris ibn 'Ali.*—In his time was the war with Sultan Abd ul Jalil the son of the daughter of Gargar. He died at Alo. He reigned fifty-three (thirty-three) years.

---

* *i.e.*, he was deposed by Ali Ghaji Dunamami and in the Blau MS. is said to have died at Makada or Màkida, *i.e.*, Northern Kordofan, to which most of the princes of the Daud branch seem ultimately to have fled. The Girgam has 'Malakata' a corruption of Màkita, *i.e.*, country of the Amakitan (Tuwareg).

55. *The Sultan Muhammad ibn Idris.*—A very handsome man and very patient. He died at Dagana. He reigned sixteen years and seven months. How great was his beneficence! So that in his time envious and malicious tongues were silent. May God reward him with happiness.

56. *The Sultan Ibrahim.*—His mother was the Gumsu (Queen). She was of the house of the Magaram. He died at N'gazargamu. He reigned seven years and seven months.

57. *The Sultan Haj Umr ibn Fasam.*—He reigned nineteen years nine months. He died at N'gazargamu.

58. *The Sultan 'Ali ibn Haj Umr.*—A warrior of great ability. In his time was the famine called Dala Dama. He died at N'gazargamu and ruled forty years. **Circa 1645-1684.**

59. *The Sultan Idris ibn 'Ali.*—Reigned twenty years.

60. *The Sultan Dunama ibn 'Ali.*—In his time was the great famine of seven years' duration. He died at N'gazargamu and reigned nineteen years. **Circa 1704-1722.**

61. *The Sultan Haj Hamdun ibn Dunama.*—His reign was one of peace and prosperity and devotion to study. He died at N'gazargamu and reigned fourteen years.

62. *The Sultan Muhammad ibn Haj Hamdun.*—In his time there occurred the famine called Ali Shuwa which lasted two years. He died at N'gazargamu and reigned sixteen years.

63. *The Sultan Dunama Gana.*—Thus was he. In his time was a severe famine. He died at N'gazargamu and reigned two years.

64. *The Sultan 'Ali ibn Al Haj Dunama*—was among the just and good. His time was famous for its love of learned men. He died at N'gazargamu. **Circa 1755-1793.**

65. *The Sultan Ahmad ibn 'Ali.*—He was a Sultan who helped the learned and aided Muslims. He was a God-fearing man. He died at N'gazargamu after reigning seventeen years. **Circa 1793-1810.**

66. *The Sultan Dunama ibn Ahmad.*—In his time he was the manliest of the manly, incomparable in appearance. He died at N'gala after reigning eight years. Peace.

KANURI GIRGAM OF THE MAGUMI MAIS (SULTANS) IN POSSESSION OF MAI MUFIO.

Transliteration.	*Translation.*
1. Mai Saibu Aisami Yemenma, Kurguli Bula Yemenbe, shiye fanze bula Yemenin kargo.	Mai Saibu whose mother was Aisa, the Mai of Yemen, the Lion of the town of Yemen; he is at his house in the town of Yemen.
2. Tatanze Ibrahima Saibumi, shiye fanze bula Yemenbin kargo.	His son Ibrahima son of Saibu: he is at his house in the town of Yemen.
3. Mai Dugu Bremi; Yeri Arbasanin.	Mai Dugu son of Brem: (he is at) Yeri Arbasan.
4. Fune Dugumi: Gage Galainin.	Fune, son of Dugu: (he is at) Gage Galai.
5. Artso Funemi: Galambutan kargo.	Artso, son of Fune: he is at Galambuta.
6. Katuri Artsomi: Guyugam Kurnawalan.	Katuri, son of Artso: (he is at) Guyugam Kurnawa.
7. Boyoma Katurimi: bula Yonin kargo.	Boyoma, son of Katuri: he is at the town of Yo.

3. *Yeri Arbasan*—see introduction.

4. *Galainin*—Some copies have Galaknin—*i.e.*, N'galaka in Borgu and it is very probable that such is the meaning. The root word in both cases in N'gal (Ingel)—ak or ek being the Tuwareg termination "people." One girgam has "Muli Funiyawan."

5. *Galambuta* has the epithet "buniramnin" "of fishes" in other copies. It probably stands for N'gala Butte or M'bute.

6. *Guyugam*—in other copies Kaigam Kurnawan; said to be the Alo region near Maiduguri but that is improbable, and it is more likely that it means the 'south' of Borku, *i.e.*, Fittri region.

7. *Yo*—*i.e.*, the Yo on the north shores of Lake Fittri, if not an older Yo in Borku. His mother (vide the Diwan) was apparently a daughter of the Mek (Mai) of Shebina (Samina) on the Wadi Batha in Wadai, then the capital of the Dajo, a branch of whom, settled along with the Bulala near Lake Fittri were and still are called Kuka (the Gaoga of Leo Africanus). According to Barth the Bulala Kingdom in Fittri was begun by one Jil (Abdul Jalil) Sikumami, whom the Diwan states to have been descended from Ume Jilmi.

It is noticeable that a title of the N'gazargamu Mais of the 16th century was "Arjiku Siku Mâkidâbe." There seems to be some connection of the official titles Shikama (Chikama) Shiruma (Chiroma) with this title of the Mais Siku (Shiku) while Arjiku seems connected with the title Arjino-ma and perhaps Arki, Arrigwa, etc.

The Bagharmi people call the Kanuri Biyo or Boyo and the Bulala they call Biyo-Bulala, while the Logone people call the modern Kanuri 'bille Ngare' (N'gale). The people of Bagharmi are called by the latter Mokkode which may be derived from Magge (Magumi) or Makada (Mâkida).

Magumi Mais (Sultans).

Transliteration.	*Translation.*
8. Bulu Boyomami: Kirzumma Ngelewalan kargo.	Bulu, son of Boyoma: he is at the town of the Dum Palms and Palm Leaves.
9. Mai Aril Arigwabe, Arigu Bulumi: Zaila Wuzulan kargo.	The Mai who was the silk of the Arigwa, Arigu son of Bulu: he is at Zaila Wuzula.
10. Mai Sho Rigumi: Kutushi Kauwalan.	Mai Sho, son of Rigu: (he is at) Kutushi of the Rocks.
11. Jil Shomi, Masr Mashidiwalan kargo.	Jil, son of Sho: (he is in) Egypt of the Mosques.
12. Ume Jilmi: Ruwaya Mashidiwalan.	Ume, son of Jil: (he is at) Ruwaya of the Mosques.
13. Dunama Umemi: Barambushi Buniramnin kargo.	Dunama, son of Ume: he is at Barambushi the town of Fishes.
14. Dalla Dunamami: bula Gam Tilo Jilargelan kargo.	Dalla, son of Dunama: he is at Jilarge (his) only town.
15. Kale Bikurmi: Bibisi Kurnawalan.	Kale, son of Bikur: (he is at) Bibisi of the "kurna" trees.
16. Tsilim Bikurmi: Bibisi Ngiziriwalan.	Tsilim, son of Bikur: (he is at) Bibisi of the "Ngiziri" trees.
17. Mai Dunama Dabalemi Tsilimarambe, Duna zau kanuro zau'o, Duna kanu Madabarbe: bula Zantamnin kargo.	Mai Dunama son of Dabale of the daughter of Tsilim, Duna who was fiercer than fire, Duna the fire of Madabar: he is at the town of Zantam.
18. Mai Kadai Matalami, Matala Boyomarambe: Yamdi Kauwa, Kurkuriwa, Zuwi Zuwi Dabinowa, Babirnin kargo.	Mai Kadai son of Matala, Matala daughter of Boyoma: he is in Yam the land of rocks, the fruitful land, the land of dates, at Zuwi Zuwi Babir.
19. Tolomarama Kashim Biri Dunamami: Biri Ukume Kulugunin kargo.	The king of Tolomaram, Kashim, Biri, son of Dunama, Biri: he is Ukume of the Pool.

---

12. Both Ume and Biri are names given to kings whose real names is Othman. This is done because, Othman being the name of one of the four rightly directed Caliphs it is considered better to avoid using it in public. This custom is very common in the Sudan.

13. *Dunama*—All Mais called Muhammad are also called Dunama and *vice versa*. The name is apparently a compound of Dun (in Kanuri "power," "might"), and Aman (*i.e.*, Ammon) the Barbar God.

14. *Dalla*—A mistake for Biri.

15. *Kale or Dalla* = Abd Allah.

16. *Bibisi*—Fifisi.

18. *Yamdi*—*i.e.*, Borku and the region to the north of it.
Babir—*i.e.*, of the Barbars.

Transliteration.	*Translation.*
20. Mai Jitku Jilwabe, Jil Kalemi: Kurguli bula Yemenbe, shiye fanze bula Yemenin kargo.	Mai who knew the Jilwa, Jil son of Kale: the Lion of the town of Yemen: (he is at) his house in the town of Yemen.
21. Kale Bikurmi Birimi, Gaduram Njimi Gawalalan kargo.	Kale son of Bikur son of Biri: he is at Gaduram Njimi Gawala (Kawal).
22. Mai Tsilim Awami Bidamarambe: Ndubu Garulan.	Mai Tsilim whose mother was Awa daughter of the Bidama: (he is at) Ndubu the walled town.
23. Kore lagatu Galewalan.	One of them (is at) Galewa.
24. Kore kuratu, kesa Ngelewabin kargo.	The chief Kore is at Kesa Ngelewa.
25. Kore lagatu Guguwalan:	One of them (is at) Guguwa.
26. Mai Idirisa Ashami: Nguru dandal ngilawa Gulurulan kargo.	Mai Idirisa whose mother was Asha: he is at Nguru with the good 'dandal' at Guluru.
27. Mai Daudu Nigale Gana: Jitwanin.	Mai Daudu, son of Nigale: (he is at) Jitwa.
28. Usumana Daudumi: Bur Tsilim Gawalalan kargo.	Usumana son of Daudu: he is at Bur Tsilim Gawala (Kawal).
29. Mai Ume Aisa Gana: Ngalbiwanin.	Mai Ume, son of Aisa: (he is at) Ngalbiwa.
30. Saibu Ganatu: Badani Ngurulan.	Saibu the Less: (he is at) Badani Nguru.

20. The identification of this **Mai** with Ibrahim Nigalemi is doubtful.
Jilwa—i.e., descendants of Jil (Abd ul Jalil) father of Ume.
Klemi or *Kalemi* may stand for N'galemi (Nigalemi).
The Kanem Kingdom is often called Yaman or Yemen.

21. Here *Bikurmi* is an epithet in memory of No. 15. The Mai was Abd Allah son of Biri.

22. *N'dubu*, i.e., D'difu near Dikwa, a very old " So " town.

25. i.e., Muhammad, Guguwa may be Leo Africanus' Gaoga, i.e., Fittri (Kuka).

26. *Ashami*—a mistake for Hafsami or Amsami. *Nguru* simply means " walled city," i.e., Njimi.

27. This *Jitwa* lies south of Malfe in Fittri.

29. *Ume*—Othman.

30. *Saibu Saif* or *Said* all mean that the name of the Mai was such that the title " Said " could be applied to it. In this case the Mai's name was Abu Bakr, so he is called " Saibu (Said) after the 1st Caliph of Islam, Abu Bakr.
Ganatu probably connotes Lagatu, i.e., he only reigned a short time.

Transliteration.	Translation.
31. Jimarama Mai Umar Idirisimi: Jimaranze Beltebin kargo.	The king of Jimara, Mai Umar, son of Idirisi: he is at his town of Jimara Belte (Belte=Hausa Hantsi, *i.e.*, 9 a.m.)
32. Isubu Saibumi: Arjino Gawalalan kargo.	Isubu, son of Saibu: he is at Arjino Gawala (Kawal).
33. Mai Mohommadu Idirisimi: Magi Zabatam kirzuma Ngelewalan kargo.*	Mai Mohommadu son of Idirisi: he is at Magi Zabatam of the Dum Palms and Palm Leaves.
34. Biri Aminami: Bagharmi Kunguwanin kargo.	Biri, son of Amina: he is at Bagharmi Kunguwa.
35. Mai Kore: lagatu Afuno Dallawalan.	Mai Kore: one of them (is at) Afuno Dallawa.
36. Mai Kagu Umar Gana: Galambutan.	Mai Kagu son of Umar: (he is at) Galambuta.
37. Dagumo Kumkumwama, Dalla Umar Gana, Dagumo Kumkumwanin kargo.	The king of Dagumo of the "kumkum" bushes. Dalla son of Umar, he is at Dagumo of the "kumkum" bushes.
38. Mai Daril Kalinwama: Kalinwanin kargo.	Mai Daril of Kalinwa: he is at Kalinwa.
39. Mai Daril Kalinwama: Kalinwa Njimi kargo.	Mai Daril of Kalinwa: he is at Kalinwa Njimi.
40. Dunama Dabalemi Burzilimwama: Burzilim Gawalalan kargo.	Dunama Dabalemi king of Burzilim son of Dabale: he is at Burzilim Gawala (Kawal).
41. Mohommadu Gaudimi: Buniwanin kargo.	Mohommadu son of Gaudi: he is at Buniwa (the town of Fishes).

32. In other Girgams he is called Saifu Saifumi—*i.e.*, he was the son of Abu Bakr, not a usurper as Barth thought.

33. Only three sons of Idris Nigalemi reigned and the identification of the other two appears fairly certain. It seems therefore that the Mohammadu Idirisimi of the Girgam can only be the Kadai Afanu ibn Idris of the Diwan.

* This is probably wrong owing to confusion with (43) and should be Mai Kadai Afunu Idirisimi, Gaduram N'jimi Gawalalan Kargo.

34. There was no kingdom of Bagharmi at this time and Kunguwan is seemingly the Kanantu of the Diwan. The Kanantu are possibly the same as the Kananiyin of Iman Ahmad and were perhaps ruled by a "descendant of Bikur" Bikurmi as Jirima (clan head).

38-39. Kalinwa is probably the equivalent of Nigalewa, which is seemingly a metathesis of N'gal-wa or N'gal-aga. The meaning is thus that they died in the region of N'galagati (Geidam district) much as the Diwan states. The Daud family in particular seem to have been called **Kalinwa**.

40. *Dabalemi*—simply an honorific title of this **Mai**.

Transliteration.	Translation.
42. Mai Mohammadu Falakma: Damkarimrilan.	Mai Mohommadu of Falak: he is at Damkarimri.
43. Mohommadu Kadaimi: magi Zabatam Kirzimma Ngelewalan kargo.	Mohammadu, son of Kadai: he is at Magi Zabatam of the Dum Palms and Palm Leaves.
44. Mai Arri Gaji Zainami, Arri Kange bula Bulalabe, bulanze Bulala Gawalalan kargo.	Mai Arri Gaji son of Zainam, Arri the smoke of the town of the Bulala: he is at his town Bulala Gawala.
45. Usumana Kadaimi: Malakatalan.	Usuman son of Kadai: (he is at) Malakata.
46. — —	—
47. Mohommadu Barambazama: Barambazalan kargo.	Mohommadu of Barambaza: he is at Barambaza.
48. Mai Arri Dunamami: Gasr Gomolan.	Mai Arri, son of Dunama: (he is at) Gasr Gomo.
49. Dunama Arrimi: Ngiswanin kargo.	Dunama son of Arri: he is at Ngiswa.

42. The title *Falakma* is very interesting and the *Damkarimrilan* makes his identification fairly certain since it means ' among the Dankir ' (or Dagara), *i.e.*, in the district of the Yarima (Yarimiya or Yamia).

Falak must be the equivalent either of Balagi (Balge), Belaka, near the Siggidim and Kauwar oases or Barâk in the Wadi Barâk between Kanem and Borku.

The Arabic writer Idrisi relates that shortly before his time 1150 A.D. the " Sahib Balak," *i.e.*, ruler of Balak who was " a vassal of the king of Nubia," raided Samina (Shebina or Sama) in the Fittri region and dispersed the inhabitants. Samina at the time was occupied by " Tajowin idolaters " (Dajo). The Orientalist Dozy in his edition of Idrisi conjectures that Balak stands for ' Pilak,' *i.e.*, the island of Philae, near Aswan on the Nile, but the idea is far-fetched and improbable.

At Idrisi's date Belaka in the Siggidim oasis could hardly have been of sufficient importance to possess a chief with an army which could raid the Dajo and in fact the capital of the Kauwar oasis was at that time Jawan.

It appears then that either Balagi (Balge) or Barâk is meant. In fact they both come to much the same thing while apparently the Kanuri variant of the name was the same as the Egyptian form of it ' Pilák ' (Falak).

The fact that the Barbar (Bar-âk) desert peoples East of the Tibesti range were, before the time of Idrisi, largely Christians and as such subject to the Meks or Kings of Dongola, seems to clinch the matter.

44. This was probably the first or original " Arri Ghaji Zeinami "—the others, *i.e.*, (48) and (51) were called so—but very likely their actual mothers were not called Zeinam at all.

46. Umr ibn Abd ul Lahi—omitted in the Girgam—perhaps because he was merely the nominee of Ali Dunamami.

47. *Barambaza*—Barbar.

49. As there was only one son of Arri who ruled, *i.e.*, Idris, this must be he—though it is unusual to call an ' Idris ' Dunama. *Ngiswa* and *Walam* are in the same region—the present Shani district on the Hawral river near Biu.

Transliteration.	Translation.
50. Mohommadu Dunamami: Gulurulan. Dunama Aminami.	Mohommadu son of Dunama: (he is at) Gurulu. Dunama son of Amina).
51. Ali Gaji Zainami: shiye bula Zantamnin kargo.	Ali Gaji whose mother was Zainam: he too is at the town of Zantam.
Arri Fanami Ngumarami, Arri Garu Kage Karuruma, Garunze Karurun kargo. (Ancestor of the Mufioma).	Arri son of Fana of the Nguma tribe, Arri king of the walled town of Kage Karuru: he is in the walls of Karuru.
52. Mohommadu (Dunama) Fanami Ngumarami: shiye fanze Gasr Gomobin kargo.	Mai Mohommadu whose mother was Fana of the Nguma tribe: he is at his house in Gasr Gomo.
53. Dalla Bikurmi Dunamami: shiye fanze Gasr Gomobin kargo.	Dalla son of Bikur son of Dunama: he is at his house in Gasr Gomo.
Aisa Kili, Ngirmaramma, Aisa Magaram Dunamaram, Maida: Mar Kingarwan kargo.	Aisa Kili Ngirmaramma, Aisa whose mother was a princess daughter of Dunama, chief of women: she is at Mar of the "Gabbarua" trees.
54. Mai Idrisa Arrimi Amsami Kime: Garunze Kimewa, bulawanze Tsadu Tsiron, kauwa dubu miyanin megun, Alaunin kargo.	Mai Idrisa, son of Arri, son of Amsa, the fair, the walls of whose town were red, who had towns in Tchad (and) thousand a hundred and ten rocks: he is at Alau.
55. Tatanze Mohommadu Fanami Bogolmarambe, Kurguli Idirisimi: Daniski bula Kanemnin kolzai.	His son Mohommadu whose mother was Fana of Bogol the Lion, son of Idirisi: he was left at Daniski a town of Kanem.

50. 'N'giswanin Kargo' is added in the text but this is an obvious error; confusion has arisen here and the words *Ngiswanin kargo* are repeated from 49 by mistake.

52. *Arri Fanami—Mommodu Fanami*—The story is that a certain N'guma woman had a son Arri Ngummama, and that when her husband died she married Mai Dunama Aminami the ruler of Bornu. To him she bore a son who afterwards became Mai Dunama Mohammadu N'gumarami. After Mai Dunama's death Mohammadu was yet only a boy. Presumably after the death of 'Ali Gaji, Arri Ngummama ruled as regent for a few years. When Mohammadu was considered old enough to succeed to the throne Arri left the capital and went to the neighbourhood of Mufio and there founded a town Kage Karuru. Some of his followers at the same time founded Mufio, which afterwards became the chief town of Arri's settlement. On Arri's death one of his sons, disappointed of the Mufio headship, went South to Mige and founded a town there.

53. Again *Bikurmi* is a 'title.'

54. *Aisa Kili*—i.e., the Magira (Queen mother) regent for Idris Alooma.

Transliteration.	Translation.
56. Tata Biskumabe Gumsumibe, Bisku Ngalagatima, Zamanzin dallan chamma Karigimulan chamma: ningili tilowa kembigila tulurwa, Gumsumi Gumsu Gremarambe, Mai Brem Gumsumi fanze Ngalagatibin kargo.	The son of the King of Bisku whose mother was Gumsu, the king of Bisku Ngalagati in whose time young he-goats gave milk, he-camels gave milk; one rainy season produced seven harvests; son of Gumsu the Gumsu whose father was Grema, Mai Brem son of Gumsu: he is at his house in Ngalagati.
57. Kirkir binabe, Bambaram sube, Dusuguma Dusu Mai Alâ Jilargebe Pusami Mai Umar Mele Gana shiye fanze Gasr Gomobin kargo.	The Mai who made men like a ball of chaff (a reference to this Mai's strict rule) a shade made of iron, the king of Dusugu the ' Dusu ' of Mai Alâ of Jilarge the great son of Pusam, Mai Umar son of Mele: he is at his house in Gasr Gomo.
58. Arri Walam deguwa Walatan uguwa, Arri bula Saube: shiye Mananzatin kolzai.	Arri of the four towns of Walam and the five towns Walata, Arri of the Sau town: he is left at Mananzati.
59. Mai Gambaruma Mataragenma, kime, Mai Mele Arri Gana: shiye Zaila Turagenin kolzai.	The king of Gambaru and of Mataragen the fair, Mai Mele son of Arri: he is left at Zaila Turagen.
60. Mai Girtigene Kunduruwa, Adawan Dawama Zatemerambe, kire, kabin ngadawa: Bugua Kurnawa Ngirmaram Karuran kargo.	The Mai (whose bounty was) like rain that comes without tornado, whose mother was Adawan Dawamazate the generous but one who dealt out death freely (reference to the Mai's fondness for war): he is at Kurura a town (once) full of horses (now) a town of ashes and " kurna " trees.
61. Mai Gidigan Gasr Gomoma, Mai Mohommadu Aji: shiye fanze Gasr Gomobin kargo.	The Mai who had Gasr Gomo to the East of him, Mai Mohommadu Aji: he is at his house in Gasr Gomo.
62. Mai Gidigan Malambuma, Mai Mohommadu Aji: shiye fanze Gasr Gomobin kargo.	The Mai who had Malambu to the East of him, Mai Mohommadu Aji: he is at his house in Gasr Gomo.

57. *Mele*—stands for Idris—just as Dunama does generally for Muhammad.

62. Generally called in Bornu Mommadu Ajimi (*i.e* Hâiimi).

Magumi Mais (Sultans).

Transliteration.	Translation.
63. Kori Lefiyami, Duna Aman Gana, shiye fanze Gasr Gomobin kargo.	The short Mai, whose mother was Lefiya, Duna son of Aman: he is at his house in Gasr Gomo.
64. Tata Dunama Lefiyamibe, Fararima Lefiyamibe, Jaji: fanze Sansanwabin kargo.	The son of Dunama son of Lefiya, Lefiya of Farari Jaji: he is at his house at Sansanwa.
65. Tatanze Haza Gana: shiye fanze Sansanwabin kargo.	His son Haza the Less: he is at his house at Sansanwa.
66. Tsilim Fune Bulwa, Duna Faranduma: Ngala Garunin kargo.	The dark skinned Mai who had a white turban, Duna king of Farandu: he is at the walled town of Ngala.
67. Mai Ngeleruma, Gumsumi Gumsu Amina Talbarambe: shiye fanze Bulangwabin kargo.	Mai Ngeleruma son of Gumsu, Gumsu Amina daughter of Talba: he is at his house in Bulangwa.
68. Burra Sugu Murge, Aman Gana, Kukawa tsironin kargo.	Burra (Ibram), Sugu Murge, (a nickname for a man named Burra) son of Aman: he is in Kukawa.
69. Tata Burra Amanmi Gana Dalatumi: Ngeletsiro Minargelan kargo.	The son of Burra son of Aman son of Dalatu: he is among the Dum Palm leaves of Minarge.

64. Sansanwa, *i.e.*, at war in a camp.
67. *N'geleruma* ruled at Kabila near Mongonu.
68. *i.e.*, Ibrahim titular Mai 1818-1846.
69. *Ali Dalatumi*—killed in battle against Shehu Umar after the Wadai invasion of 1846.

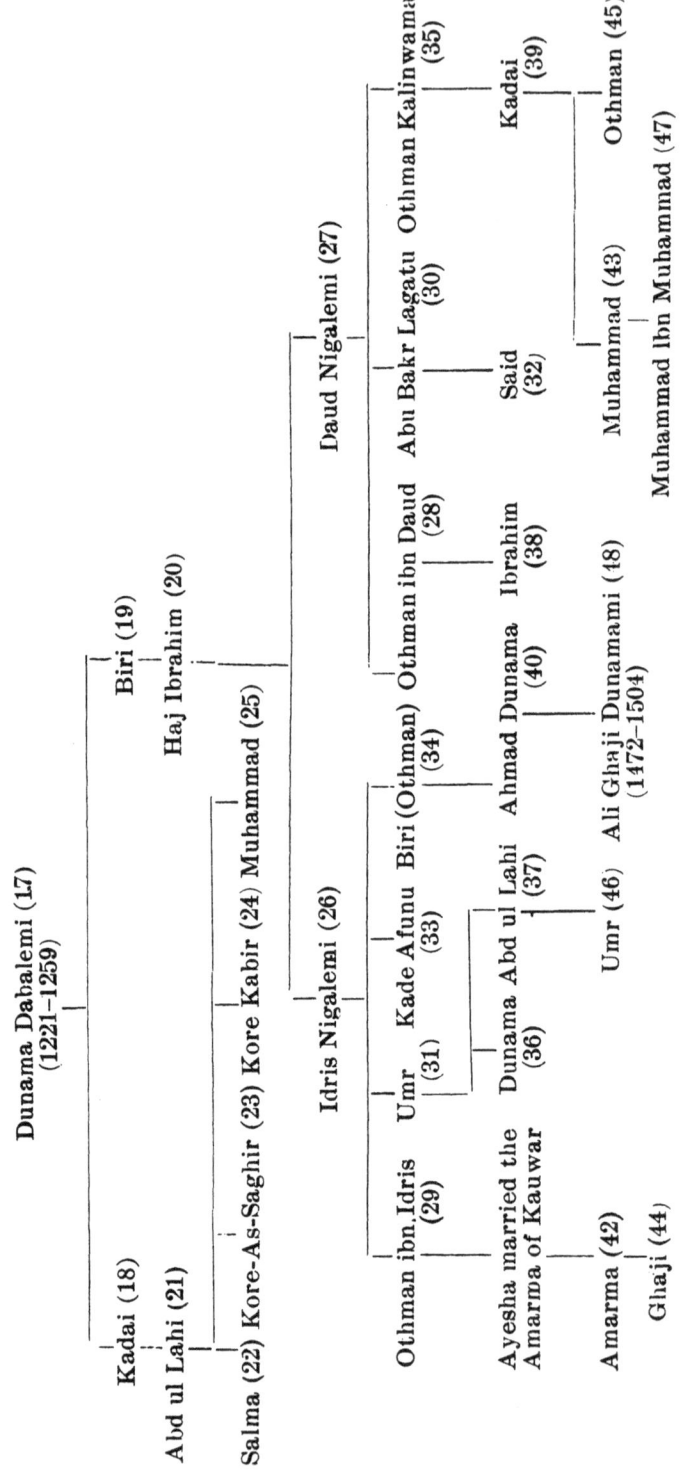

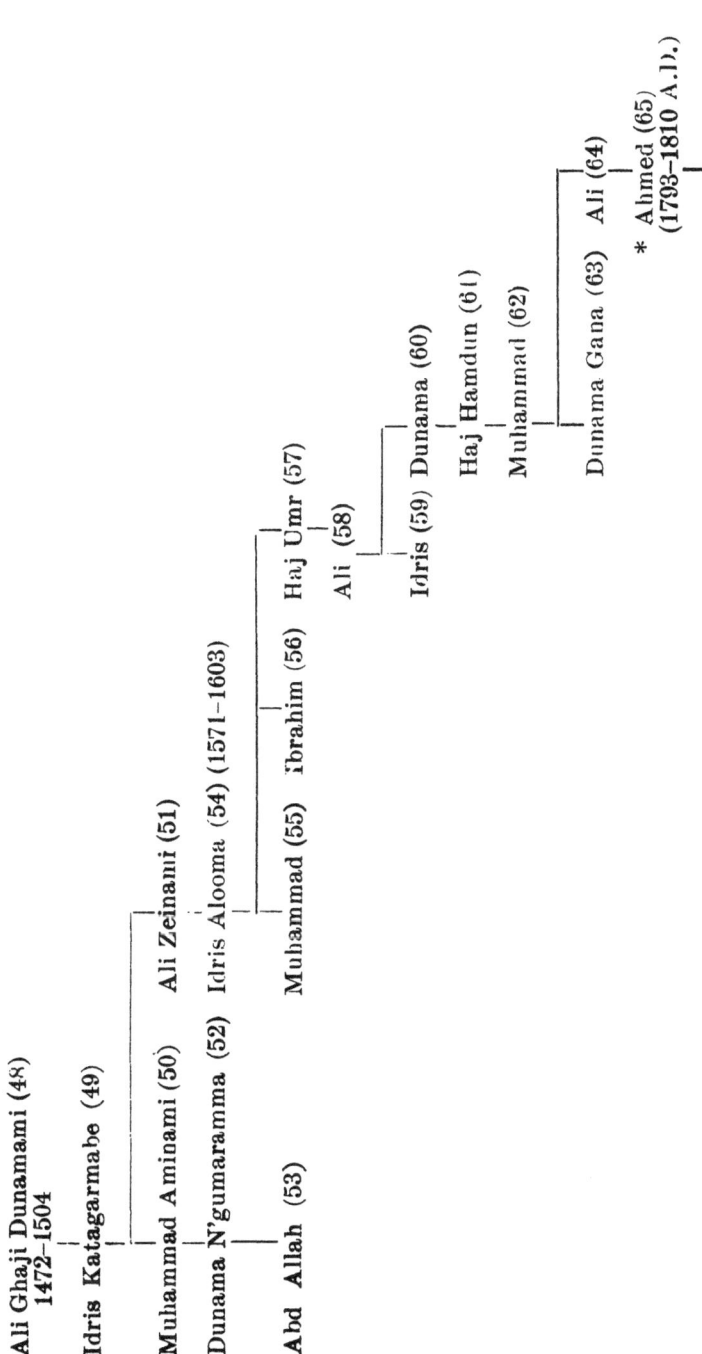

Note.—* From him descend the family of the late Maina Gumsumi, Mallam Husein of Marte and other Magumi in Bornu. The present Emirs of Lafia (Nasarawa), descend from (64) Ali.

NOTE ON THE EARLY BARBAR CULTS OF THE SAHARA AND SUDAN.

(GIRGAM No. 17).

Mai Dunama Dabalemi, Tsilimarambe Duna Zau Kanuro Zau'o, Duna Kannu Madabarbe, bula Zantamnin Kargo.
" King Dunana son of Dabale the daughter of Tsilim: Duna " who was fiercer than fire. Duna the fire of Madabar. He lies at " the town of Zantam ".

So runs part of the Kanuri Girgam, giving the names of the rulers of Bornu since the beginning, the part referring to Mai (King) Dunama Dabalemi who ruled Kanem and the Teda country 1221-1259 A.D.

The word Madabar is in different versions transcribed as Mutabar, Matabas and Mutabas.

Modern Kanuri say that it is a corruption of the Arabic word ' murtaba ' and means shedîd, *i.e.*, " a very hot fire ". They say that the expression ' kannu murtaba ' is an expression which means a formidable or awesome fire.

This explanation is not altogether convincing, because—
- (a) it is unlikely that an Arab derivative of this kind would have been incorporated with the Kanuri language at an early date;
- (b) though metathesis of consonants is common enough there seems no reason why an ' r ' should be transposed in this way.

On the other hand, the fact that the sense of ' murtaba ' is assigned as the sense of the word is curious since—
- (a) the derivatives of the verb ' rataba ' in Arabic bear the sense of ' ritual ', religious service, office, etc.;
- (b) as applied to fire therefore it could hardly be said to mean anything, unless it meant a ritual fire of some sort.

Since, however, it is stated that at one time the ancestors of the Kanuri and Teda worshipped ' fire '—though, naturally, that is not admitted by modern Muslim Bornu, in connection with its rulers—it seems most probable that ' murtaba ' is a bowdlerised substitute for some word, not unlike it perhaps, which has the same connotation not in regard to the religion of Islam, but to the preceding ' fire worship '.

The accompanying table gives the words used for ' fire ' and ideas cognate to it, in the five principal Barbar languages of the Sudan belt, Hausa, Tamashek, Kanuri, Tebu and Fulfulde.

Of these languages, Fulfulde and Tebu are probably the oldest in their present form. They seem to represent the language of the pre-Tuwareg inhabitants of the Sahara, the Gara races.

Kanuri, one must suppose, was developed from Teda or something akin to it, while Hausa represents a linguistic stratum, possibly at one time akin to the proto-Teda languages, but which was radically reformed and changed by the influence of Tamashek, which itself, it would appear, borrowed many words from the pre-existing Teda-Gara languages.

To the primitive Pullo (Fulani) the sun (a female) had the same name as they gave to their cattle—a cow being 'nagge', the sun 'nange.' Nan is the name of the Supreme Deity among many of the tribes who lived in what was the area of Kororafa supremacy, and in the form Tanit was the Carthaginian name for the Barbar Inna (mother) who was equivalent to the Tyrian Astarte or Ashtareth. Astarte in turn was a local adaptation of the Babylonian Ishtar or Nana, the sun goddess whose statue at Erech in Chaldea, was carried away as early as 2280 B.C. by the Elamites under Kudurnakhundi.

There also developed in Chaldea the famous city of Ur, the place of the worship of the moon god, which was worshipped under the name of 'Nannar' or 'Nanak'.

Coming to the name for moon in Fulfulde, it is apparently the name common to Tebu and Tamashek, ori or ayor, to which is prefixed an 'l' which looks very like the Semitic definite article. This same root is clearly responsible for the Fulfulde name Yero and the Hausa word Yaro, which means a 'boy.'

The similarity of ori or ayor to Ur is noticeable, while in Kanuri 'Nannari' would mean 'place of Nan', and in Tamashek Nanak, would mean 'son of Nan'.

The Hausas and Fulani believed that the moon was a boy and the sun his mother. In Teda it is noticeable that the word for sun 'zi' or 'ze' is similar to the Sumerian word 'zi' which meant the indwelling spirit of life which every natural object had.

In Teda this root 'zi' is responsible for the words for "heat of the day" and "smoke" as also their word for "sandals", i.e., izzi, which may mean that there was a connection between the wearing of shoes, and the presence of fire or smoke. Also it may be that this 'zi' root is cognate to the Tebu word for star 'teske' and the Hausa words for 'heat' and 'morning', viz., zafi and safi and 'light' haske.

The Fulfulde word for simple fire is 'iti' which may or may not be connected with the Tuwareg caste of semi-priests called Ite-san or Ite-seyen. The word for 'eye' in Fulfulde is itere, plural yitere, and 'eye-ball' is tamne yitere. In Tamashek, eye is têt plural tittawin, and 'eye' in Hausa is ido.

In Tamashek eribbe plural iraben is 'eye-ball'.

It would seem possible from a comparison of these forms that the Tamashek tara 'to burn' (of the sun) is compounded of ite and a root Ra or Re which originally meant the eyeball or pupil of the eye, and hence that the Tamashek itarar and Hausa tamrari, 'stars' originally meant 'eyes of fire' while fu or hu, (f)hod or fut, meant the action of emission of light or beams, whence Tamashek tara-hod, heat of day, (Ful) hod-ere star, Tamashek hod 'smoke' and efeu (fire), tahist (flame), tafuk (sun), tafaut (light), and tifaut (morning) and Hausa 'fura' to blow or ignite, and 'fudo' 'to come forth' of the sun.

We may even perhaps, tentatively, postulate as the primitive cosmographical terminology of the proto-Barbar, the forms:—

Nan—mother (the sun).
Re or Ra—orb or disc of the sun, moon, stars, or fire.
Hu or fu—the active principle or beams of the sun, moon, stars, or fire.
Te or ite—the eye.
Ze or Izze—the immanent force of the sun causing heat, fire, etc.
Ur—the moon.

The analogy between these simple Barbar terms and the terminology of the God-names of the Semitic world in general from Babylon onwards, as also that of Egypt, is somewhat striking. In general, it cannot well be mere coincidence even if a percentage of the comparisons made are fallacious for one reason or another.

It is improbable that this African nomenclature was taken to Egypt and Asia. The inference therefore is, that these terms came to Africa from Asia and Egypt, with the corollary that the European occupation of Africa is only the last of cultural occupations which have been pushing their way West and South, for at least 5,000 years, occupations which came ultimately from Asia and which introduced to Africa the cosmic and religious conceptions from time to time current among the great nations of antiquity.

Such literary evidence for this as exists in the Sudan, is—

(a) the historical or quasi-historical records in Arabic as exist particulary in Bornu;
(b) a chronicle of the Kings of Kano also in Arabic.

From the former, it is apparent that the early Barbars (Zaghawa) of Kanem set great store by a box or 'ark' which contained the 'sacra' of the tribe, compared by the Muslim chroniclers to the Jewish 'ark of the covenant' and said to have been a sikîna (shekina) or 'glory'. The 'sacrum' was called 'mune'—a name which among the Kanembu becomes Mani or Man, the mythical ancestor of several tribes, and is clearly the same as the Tamashek 'amane' (Aman) God, which is compounded with 'akel' earth, to form the word Amen-okal 'king' or 'head of the tribe.' Similarly the 'Apa', the ruling caste of the people called Kwona or Kororafa, who are now called Jukon, had a box containing 'sacra' called aba-kindo. The first part of this word is 'apa' i.e., the ruling race or tribe itself, and the latter part is probably the Barbar kinda or kinta, i.e., mother, which came to mean 'sacra'.

Abakindo was able, like the Ark of the Covenant, to part rivers and is said to have done so on various occasions. Among the 'Apa' the Supreme God was Asi-don (Achi-don) and his right hand minister was 'Amma' the variant Barbar word for 'mother' (Inna), while the God who corresponded to Osiris or Adonis was called Gioñ or Joñ.

It would seem that in the 'Apa' language 'chi' or 'si' was the same as the modern 'chio' (chuo) and meant 'great'.

'Don' on the other hand, is, most probably, the Kanuri 'Dun', Tebu 'Dunore' which means 'strength' in the Royal pre-Muslim Kanuri name Dun-ama of which a variant was Ark-ama (Ar-ki or Ariki), and 'Kadaba' which, in Kanuri, means 'a hawk'. We may also, perhaps, compare the Fulfulde word for sky 'do' or 'du'.

If it is assumed, as may well be the case, having regard to the close connection between the Kanuri Mais (Kings) and the Nile Valley, that Ark-ama is the Merotic name transliterated by the Greeks Erganenes, it would seem reasonable to suppose that Dun-ama is a name of the same type, and means the 'power of Amma', the word 'Duna' being either a derivative of the Semitic Adon 'Lord' or a form of the same root.

It would seem, also, that both at Bepi and Wukari, the capitals of the 'Apa', and among the tribes of the Chad region in pre-Islamic times, the following elements were closely associated in worship:—

(1) Worship of a 'ram-god' called at Wukari 'Amma' and in the Chad region 'Mani'.
(2) Worship of trees, or a tree, or grove.
(3) Worship of 'big rocks' or high places (Dalla).
(4) An island, as the venue of worship.
(5) Worship of fire or a fire.

As regards

(1) At Wukari (Apa), the ram-god, is called Amma, and a ram is sacrificed ritualistically once a year. In Bornu, the word for ram is N'gelaro, which suggests a comparison with the word for the 'sun' 'kingal', the -aro termination being, perhaps, the root we have already noticed, meaning disc or orb. In Hausa, a ram is 'rago', and in Fulfulde, 'jaudiri'. Jau is the commonest Fulbe prefix meaning 'great' equivalent to the Tebu 'jo', Kanuri 'zo' or 'zu', and Apa 'chu' or 'chio'.

In Tebu, it is said that, while an ordinary ram is called Wôna, the pagan ram-god is called Wonî, the latter form seeming to have some connection with (a) the name of the second legendary Mai of Kanem, Fune, and (b) the name of the Tuwareg mouth-covering or veil; in Kanuri, Fune.

(2) Trees—it is noticeable that in the words for tree in Hausa—'itache'; Tamashek—'ehishk' plural 'ehishkan'; Tebu—'akel'; Kanuri—'hiska'; Fulfulde—'lekki' plural ledde', the Tebu and Fulfulde forms are almost the same. The Tebu word for 'tree' being similar to the Tamashek and Kanuri forms for 'land', i.e., cultivated land; while the Tamashek and Kanuri forms for tree are similar, and like the word in Hausa, iska, which means (1) a demon or jinn (2) the wind. It is noticeable that in the Kano chronicle where a description of a sacred grove is given, the sacred tree is called by the Semitic Sun-God name—Shamuz.

(3) A name for a sacred hill or big rock throughout the western and central Sudan is Dalla or Dâla. The word seems to have existed among all the present Barbar or semi-Barbar peoples since remote antiquity. It seems cognate to the Tamashek Adar

plural Idaren = hills, and it would seem as if in ancient times, in the Chad region, the Mai-Dâla or 'owner of the hill or rock' was the Chief Priest. This sense of Dâla, it may be conjectured, is probably derived from the fact that camps of invading Barbars were usually on 'hills'. The original sense of the word or root 'dal' or 'dar', otherwise 'dir' and 'tir' or 'tal' would seem to be a circle or encampment. Among the Bornu Arabs and Kanuri of to-day, whereas a 'dirdir' means a zariba or enclosure, a doûr is a permanent camp. In the Kauwar Oasis (Tebu), the dir-de is 'chief of the dir' or encampment, whereas the encampment itself, the capital of the Oasis at one time, was Dir-ki or Dir-ku, the 'ki' standing for the Beni 'Kiye' or 'Kaye', the name of the Barbar tribes who established their rule in Kanem and Kauwar.

With Dâr the Arabic verb for circle 'dâra' and its derivative may be compared; as well as the names given to Asiatic nomads by the Egyptians, such as Da'ir or Da'ar, which the Greeks turned into Daradae, Daratitae, etc.; whence such names as Daradus flumen, etc., in the antique maps of Africa, both in the Senegal region and other parts of Northern Africa. The Daradae was perhaps the Teda or Kanuri Dar-de or 'chief of the Dar' or 'dur' or 'dir'.

The Daradae are, by classical authors, associated with the eponymous ancestors of the Blemmyes. Their name, however, both in this, its Latin form, and its Egyptian form Balhemu, is very similar to the Barbar words Bal-am or Bul-am, i.e., people called Bul or Bal, the modern Beli, who gave their name to the present chief town of the oasis of Kauwar, i.e., Bulma (place of the Bul, who were exactly the same as the Kiye or Kinin (Kindin)). The capital or chief encampment of the Kiye, in that region, was Dir-ki(n).

The Bornu title, Kachella or Kajela, in Teda Keyidala (Ketala), seems to mean the Dala-Mai or 'Lord of Dala' of the Keyi, i.e., Beni Keyi.

(4) The words for island are as follows:—

Hausa	tsibiri or chibiri.
Tamashek	autel: cf. place of pasturage = amadel; shepherd = amadân.
Kanuri	kati chiron n'jibe.
Tebu	barage.
Fulfulde	dunde.

In Hausa, the word 'tchibiri', has two meanings (1) an island, (2) a small cone made of clay or earth, similar to the masseboth of the Semites. Sacrifice of fowls, etc., are made on a 'tchibiri'.

In the Kano chronicle, the name of the God, whose shrine was on an island in the midst of the water called Jakara, which in turn was surrounded by a grove, was Tchunburburayi, which is said to be a plural form of 'tchibiri' with a Barbar personal ending. In the middle of the island was the tree 'Shamuz' the Semitic sun-god. We are also told that the grove surrounding Jakara was called Mutamma or Mat-amma, which had the same connotation, and that the 'name' (sic) of Tchunburburayi was Randaya, the Hausa word for sun (feminine) being rana.

If trouble was coming smoke would come out of the tree and island.

In Tebu, the word for mouth is 'chi'; in Kanuri 'chi-di' means 'land'. The Teda call the volcano written on maps, 'Emi Kussi' "anyi or emi (mother) wâni durdân" which means 'mother of the place of fire', in Kanuri, 'ya kannu chirobe'.

Another region in Tibesti is called Emi Madamma, the meaning of which name appears to be the same as that given to Emi Kussi. Mat (Mut) was a name of Amma or Inna 'mother' and the equivalent of Tanit 'the face of Baal', a name which is probably cognate of that of the Egyptian goddess Anait, and the Hausa name Naito (Neto).

We have seen that a form meaning mouth in Teda 'chi', with 'di' becomes 'chi-di' in Kanuri meaning 'earth', while in Hausa 'chibia' means 'the navel'. It may be that the Hausa word chi-bi-ri (island) comes from the Teda 'chi' as also 'chibia', *i.e.*, 'mouth or navel'.

Among the Apa, 'Asshe', is the name of the female counterpart of the phallic emblem (*i.e.*, the chibiri) of the God Gioñ or Joñ. Gioñ was probably, originally a female, Amma, but since the deity has become a God, the generalised word for ancestress or grandmother is Yaku, while we find in Tamashek:—

(1) asheni ... ... blood (Hausa: jini);
(2) ashiksu ... ... food (Hausa: abinchi);
(3) asherik ... ... sorcery;
(4) agadesh ... ... family;
(5) ehishk ... ... tree (Hausa: itache);
(6) asikke ... ... tomb;
(7) sikia ... ... Kanuri (siku) the Royal Family.

In Kanuri, Asshe, is a female name, apart from the Arabic Ayesha which may, or may not be connected with it. They are connected in thought by the Kanuri, just as is the name Man or Mani with Muhammad, though, in reality, the two latter are separate names having no connection in origin.

Asshe, it may be conjectured, was thus the Barbar equivalent of the Meroitic Wesh, *i.e.*, Isis, the Mother Goddess, and thus the equivalent of Tanit and Mat-amma. It may be inferred from the above that the 'sacra' called 'Sokana' and 'Dirki' which are mentioned in the Kano chronicle several times, were respectively the Sacra of the Chu-kwana (Jukon) and Dir-keyi (Zaghawa Barbars of Kanem) respectively, *i.e.*, the Mune of the Kanuri and the Aba-kindo of the Jukon.

(5) Coming back then to the 'fire of Matabar or Mutabar' its first syllable Mat or Mut is most probably the same as the Mad of Mad-amma in Emi Madamma, possibly a volcano in the region whence the invading Barbars came since the seat of their earliest settlements in Kanem was the region now called Madam or Madamma, the Matan of the Arab geographer Idrisi, which,

we may with reason suppose, meant "people of Mad or Mat, *i.e.*, the Mother Goddess".

'Abar' may be the Barbar root found in such Tamashek expressions as 'ebarbaragh' I go forth; 'ayor ebarbar' the moon came forth; 'simbara' let them loose: Shuwa Arabic 'bara' outside. The fire of 'Matabar' would then be the 'fire of a volcano'.

These fire aspects of 'cults' which were and are more or less common among the pagan tribes of the Sahara and Sudan, are well illustrated by the legend of the coming of the Barbar Dagara who are called Hausas to Kano, as narrated in "the Kano Chronicle." The legend runs as follows.

IN THE NAME OF GOD, THE MERCIFUL, THE COMPASSIONATE, MAY GOD BLESS THE NOBLE PROPHET.

This is the history of the lords of this country called Kano. Barbushe, once its chief, was of the stock of Dâla,* a black man of great stature and might, a hunter, who slew elephants with his stick and carried them on his head about nine miles. Dâla was of unknown race, but came to this land, and built a house on Dâla, hill. There he lived—he and his wives. He had seven children—four boys and three girls—of whom the eldest was Garagéje. The Garagéje was the grandfather of Buzame, who was the father of Barbushe. Barbushe succeeded his forefathers in the knowledge of the lore of Dâla, for he was skilled in the various pagan rites. By his wonders and sorceries and the power he gained over his brethren he became chief and lord over them. Among the lesser chiefs with him were Gunzago, whose house was at the foot of Gorondutse to the East. After him came Gagiwa, father of Rubu, who was so strong that he caught elephants with rope. There were also Gubanásu, Ibrahim, Bardóje, Nisau, Kanfatau, Doje, Janbére, Gamakúra, Safátaro, Hangógo, and Gartsangi. These were next to Barbushe in rank. Tsanburo lived at Jigiria, and Jandámisa at Magum. The last named was the progenitor of the Rumáwa. From Gogau to Salamta the people traced their descent from Rumá, and were called Rumáwa because they became a great people. Hambaro's house was at Tanagar. Gambarjado, who lived at Fanisau, was the son of Nisau. All these and many more there were—pagans. From Toda to Dan Bakóshi and from Doji to Dankwoi all the people flocked to Barbushe on the two nights of Idi—for he was all-powerful at the sacrificial rites.

Now the name of the place sacred to their god was Kakua.† The god's name was Tchunburburai. It was a tree called Shamuz.

---

* The name of a rock and also a man.
†Otherwise called Kagua.

The man who remained near this tree day and night was called Mai-Tchunburburai. The tree was surrounded by a wall, and no man could come within it save Barbushe. Whoever else entered, he entered but to die. Barbushe never descended from Dâla except on the two days of Idi. When the days drew near, the people came in from East and West and South and North, men and women alike. Some brought a black dog, some a black fowl, others a black he-goat, when they met together on the day of Jajibere at the foot of Dâla hill at eve. When darkness came, Barbushe went forth from his house with his drummers. He cried aloud and said " Great Father of us all, we have come nigh to thy dwelling in supplication, Tchunburburai ", and the people said: " Look on Tchunburburai, ye men of Kano! Look toward Dâla ". Then Barbushe descended, and the people went with him to the god. And when they drew near, they sacrificed that which they had brought with them. Barbushe entered the sacred place— he alone—and said: " I am the heir of Dâla, like it or no, follow me ye must, perforce ". And all the people said: " Dweller on the rock, Our Lord Amane, we follow thee perforce ". Thus they spoke and marched round the sacred place till the dawn, when they arose, naked as they were, and ate. Then would Barbushe come forth and tell them of all that would befall through the coming year, even concerning the stranger who should come to this land, whether good or ill. And he foretold how their dominion should be wrested from them, and their tree be cast down and burnt, and how this mosque should be built. " A man shall come ", said he, " to this land with an army, and gain the mastery over us ". They answered, " why do you say this? it is an evil saying ". Barbushe held his peace. " In sooth ", said he, " you will see him in the sacred place of Tchunburburai; if he comes not in your time, assuredly he will come in the time of your children, and will conquer all this country, and forget you and yours and exalt himself and his people for years to come ". Then were they exceedingly cast down. They knew well that he did not lie. So they believed him, and said: " What can we do to avert this great calamity?" He replied, " There is no cure but resignation ". They resigned themselves. But the people were still grieving over this loss of dominion at some distant time, when Bagoda*, a generation later, came with his host to Kano. There

---

* Bagoda. He was son of Bauwo son of Bayajidda, of the stock of Ham the son of Noah. It was by reason of his high lineage, that Bauwo conquered all Hausaland—he and his six sons. The first of them was Kazura; then came Bagoda, Ubandoma, Gamgama, Kumaio, and Kasanki. When Bauwo died, Kazura became Emir of Daura. This is a reliable account in a book of the names of the Emirs of Kano.

is a dispute, however. Some deny this, and say that it was Bagoda's grandson* who first reached Kano, and that he† and his son‡ died at Sheme. He, at all events, entered Kano territory first. When he came, he found none of Barbushe's men, save Janbere, Hambarau, Gertsangi, Jandamissa, and Kanfatau. These said, " Is this man he of whom Barbushe told us?" Jambere said, " I swear by Tchunburburai if you allow this people within our land, verily they will rule you, till you are of no account." The people refused to hearken to the word of Jambere, and allowed the strangers to enter the country, saying: ". Where will Bagoda find strength to conquer us?"

So Bagoda and his host settled in Garazawa and built houses there. After seven months, they moved to Sheme. The district from Jakara to Damargu was called Garazawa; from Jakara to Santolo was called Zadawa; from Santolo to Burku was called Fongui; from Banfai to Wasai was called Zaura. From Wateri to the rock of Karia was called Dundunzuru; from Santolo to Shike, Shiriya; from Damargu to Kazaure, Sheme; from Burku to Kara, Gaude; from Kara to Amnagu, Gija; from Karmashe to Ringim, Tokawa. Now the chiefs whom Bagoda found holding sway over this land acknowledged no supreme lord save Tchunburburai and the grove of Jakara. Jakara was called " Kurmin Bakkin Rua ", because its water was black, and it was surrounded by the grove§.

The pagans stood in awe of the terrors of their god and this grove, which stretched from Gorondumasa to Dausara. The branches and limbs of its trees were still—save, if trouble were coming on this land, it would shriek thrice, and smoke would issue forth in Tchunburburai, which was in the midst of the water. Then they would bring a black dog and sacrifice it at the foot of Tchunburburai. They sacrificed a black he-goat in the grove. If the shrieks and smoke continued, the trouble would indeed reach them, but if they ceased, then the trouble was stayed. The name of the grove was Matsama and the name of Tchunburburai was Randaya.

The greatest of the chiefs of the country was Mazauda, the grandfather of Sarkin Makafi. Gijigiji was the blacksmith: Bugazau was the brewer: Hanburki doctored every sickness: Danbuntunia, the watchman of the town at night, was the progenitor of the Kurmawa. Tsoron Maje was " Sarkin Samri ", and Jandodo was " Sarkin Makada Gundua da Kuru ". Beside these there was Maguji, who begot the Maguzawa, and was the miner and smelter among them.

---

* Gijinmasu.
† Bagoda.
‡ Warisi.
§ The " Ghailata " means trees.

Again there was Asanni the forefather of minstrels and chief of the dancers. Bakonyaki was the archer. Awar, grandfather of the Awrawa, worked salt of Awar. He was Sarkin Rua of this whole country. In all there were eleven of these pagan chiefs, and each was head of a large clan. They were the original stock of Kano.

1.—BAGODA, SON OF BAUWO.
A.H. 389—455.   A.D. 999—1063.

"Then came Bagoda with his host, and was the first Sarki of this land. His name was Daud. His mother's name was Kaunasu. He began by occupying Dirani for two years. Thence he moved to Barka, and built a city called Talutawa, where he reigned two years.

The names of the pagan chiefs who Bagoda met were Jankare, Biju, Buduri (who had many children—about a hundred) and Ribo. Bagoda overcame them and killed their leader Jankare. Then he came to Sheme, and found Gabusani, Bauni, Gazauri, Dubgege, Fasataro, and Bakin Bunu there. He conquered them all, and built a city, and reigned at Sheme sixty-six years."

It is evident that though this Kano chronicle purports to describe an indigenous negro cult, yet, in fact, it describes a Barbar cult which may have obtained before the invasion, or, on the other hand, may have been brought to Kano by the invaders.

Dâla, as we have seen, is an early Hamitic word for hill and camp, pronounced Dar or Tar by the more northerly races, Darkiyi being a Barbar of a 'Dar' or 'Dir' whence, in the singular, a Barbar was called a Tar-gi, of which the Arab broken plural is Tuwarek or Tawarik.

It is noticeable that the Chief of the Dâla at Kano is 'a Barbar'—Barbushi, and that his children number the Semitic sacred number seven.

He lives on the Dâla, while his lesser chief Gunzago, *i.e.*, Gumzaki (Kamzaki) 'the morning star' lives near Gorondutsi, 'the solitary hill'.

Goro, in Hausa, a 'single man' or 'bachelor' is, one may suppose, cognate to the Fulfulde Gor-ko 'man'. Dutsi 'rock' contains the same root as occurs in "Tu-bu" 'rock-people', *i.e.*, Tebu.

At the foot of Dâla, the present market place of Kano, lay Kagua or Kakua (Gagua) the locality (Chibiri) sacred to the divinity of the island in the middle of a sheet of water (Jakara) surrounded by a grove of trees (Mat-amma).

The Chibiri itself was called Randaya, and the tree in the midst of it was called Shamuz. The Barbar conqueror is called Bagod, *i.e.*, the Tebu word Bagodi which means "elder" or "chief", in Arabic "Sheikh". The Numidian name 'Bogud' found in Sallust's works may be the same word.

Kagua, it may be supposed, is the plural (Tedu-Kanuri plural) of the word still used in the Niger Valley for both (*a*) chief (*b*) an idol, *i.e.*, ' gago '.

The island is regarded as the chibia or ' navel ' of the cult, whence its name Randaya, a ' Randa ' being the large waterpot in which a household keeps its diurnal store of water, *i.e.*, water for the râna = ' day '. The Randa is, in fact, the chibia (navel) of the household water supply, just as the ' chibiri ' or ' sacred-island ' is the navel of the sacra of the people.

The whole visible sacra proceed from the Mat-amma, Great Mother*, the N. African Tanit, the outward manifestation (face of Baal) of the spirit (Baal) which inhabited the tree (Shamuz), *i.e.*, the sun-spirit.

Jakara is probably the same word as the place name Jigiria, *i.e.*, both are forms of the Tamashek *Egireu* ' steam or water '. The narrative is especially interesting as throwing light on the Carthaginian epithet of Tanit as ' pene Baal ' face of Baal, the latter being, in the case of Carthage, Melkart or Moloch (Milk).

The conception underlying the Kano cult evidently is that the Baal is ' unseen ' and ' invisible ', a conception which may account from the fact that the men, clearly Libyans, depicted on the rocks at the Wadi Telisaghe, between Murzuk (Zeila) and Ghat and described by the traveller Barth, Vol. i, p. 197, have no human faces or heads but are given the heads (*a*) of a bull, (*b*) of an apparently Egyptian deity. The tails worn by the Libyans were possibly worn for the same reason that certain pagan tribes in the Sudan now wear them, *i.e.*, owing to ram-worship, the worship of the long-tailed Saharan ram; but the substitution of animal for human heads in the picture seems to mean that the aggressor is represented with the head of the ' ram-god ', *i.e.*, Baal Ammon, while the other human figure carrying a shield like those of the Chad peoples in contrast to the big oryx shield carried by the Ammon figure, was Anubis or Anub(p), the jackal-headed son of Isis and Osiris, the ' Mallam Dilla ' or ' learned jackal ' of the Hausas. The scene seems to represent, in other words, Imoshagh (Illam or Illela) or ' nobles ' who were worshippers of Amen-Ra, the Egyptian sun-God, attacking the An-ab, Nobatae, or Anbat otherwise the N'gara or N'gala cattle-owning Kushite races, whom they found in the Sahara, at the time of their coming west from the Nile Valley.

In Tamashek, the jackal is called ' ebeg ', while a ram is ' abbegu ', both forms seemingly connected with the Tebu Bogodi =' Sheikh ' or ' Chief ', Numidian Bogud and perhaps Aryan Bogu (God).

As the form Amba or Anab is, among the Southern Teda or Tebu, commonly used to denote the more northerly Anna or Anu, *i.e.*, ' people ', it may be that it is from this form, a compound of An and the Eastern Hamitic Ab or Ba, that the various forms

---

* cf. in Tamashek masmas = grandmother.

of NEBED, said to be descriptive and mean " with hair-done-in-rat-tails ", of the Nuba, Nobatae, Anbat, Napata, etc., came, *i.e.*, that the original Nubians were races similar to the Tebu, being later called Gara or Garawan, hence Garamantes, by the Imoshagh Barbars.

There have been, at least since the 13th century, in the Gongola-Benue region of Nigeria, a caste of Barbar origin who call themselves ' Apa ' and who claim connection with Nubia. Peoples connected with them are further called Nupe or Nuffi. They are people among whom handicrafts were highly developed, and among whom craftsmen were not regarded as of inferior caste.

The Gongola region was one of their main centres of power in the middle ages; the places they inhabited are still known as Kalam, Kanan, Dugu-ri, Kun-de (Kwon-di), Gwani, Gwan-be, etc.

Further East, as late as the 16th century, these peoples appear as the stiff-necked Kananiyyin of Kanem, said to have been extirpated by Mai Idris Alooma.

By the traveller Barth, the Kananiyyin were thought to have been related to the Bongo or Haddadi (blacksmith) clans of Kanem, but it seems certain that whether this was so or not, they were not dissimilar in origin to the Kindin (Barbars of Kanem).

In the Fittri region, we find a tradition that the early inhabitants of the region were Fellata, *i.e.*, non-Semitic nomads, while in the Northern Kordofan, we come to the region called by these Apa races themselves ' Jebel Kwon ' and by the Kanuri, Makada or Makida, *i.e.*, country inhabited by Amakitan Barbars called by them Beni Kiye, or Beni Kayi, to give an appearance of Arab origin.

Kordofan is, however, the region of the legendary table of the sun and the ' noble Blemmyes ' who were of the same race as the Daradae who, in classical legend, fought under Bacchus or Hercules (Arkel). In this region also were the peoples called by the Greeks ' Makrobioi ', probably Makwaraba, which might well have been their own name for their settlement, equivalent to the Barbar and Hausa form, Kwararafa, or Kororapa.

Makrisi, the Arab writer, credits them with an ancestor, Makorri, who came from Yaman. Among the Tebu the word for Supreme God is Muguri. The Zaghawa of Wadai talk of their country as Kworra-dar. It would thus seem that the enclitic kwa- or -kor, which is found in many name compounds throughout the central and eastern Sudan must be equivalent to ' Gor ' and ' Gar ' which is, among the Fulani, the common tribal appellation for pre-Tuwareg Barbars, a still earlier Sudanese appellation for people being the syllable -ba, or -ab, -ap. To the Saharan-Gara races, as for instance, the Teda, strangers of any sort would be ' aban ' (apan) or (anab), so that when their country became subject to Asiatic invasions, those Asiatics also would be Arab or Apan.

The names ' Napata ' and ' Nobatae ' might be cited as probable examples, as also ' Nabataeans ', who were craftsmen.

The origin of the word Ethiopia itself has also not been satisfactorily settled. A derivation which suggests itself, from the train of thought followed above, is that Ethiopia stands for—

(a) the root contained in the Hausa ' wuta ' and Fulfulde ' ite ' or ' yite ' (fire);

(b) the early Barbar word for people, ' apan ' or ' aban '

It might be suggested that Aethiops stood for ' ite '—Apan fire-people ' or ' sun-worshippers ', who corresponded to the athravan ' ' fire-kindlers ' of the Zend Avesta and Iranian or Aryan peoples who followed. Zarathustra (Zoroaster), of whom the modern representatives are the Parsees, so called because they came from Fars (Persia).

It would appear that from an early date the Iranian or Aryan predatory nomads who lived in Turan were called by the Greeks *Daoi* and by other races Daha, Dana, Dahae, and then Sacae, Sycthians, and Massagetae, in Roman times.

About 1700 B.C., these races, it would seem, introduced the horse among the Turanian peoples of Irak and the Semites of Syria and probably North Africa as well as Egypt. Thus the Sanscrit word for ' to burn ' (tara) English, star, might be responsible for the first part of the word ' athravan ' and their word for horse " *aspos* " may conceivably contain the root from which the Tamashek ' ais ' plural ' iyesan ' horse, ' eshed ' donkey, etc., came, as well as the Fulfulde ' pachu '.

At the period corresponding to these great Iranian movements in Asia, the Egyptians called certain Asiatic predatory nomads, who may perhaps have been Aryans, by the name of Fenh, while the regions which the Egyptians called Punt, *i.e.*, the regions at the mouth of the Red Sea, were, at the opening of the Muslim era, very largely inhabited by peoples whom the Arabs of Oman called Ja-fun and Barbar, and apparently classed together.

The Jafun or Fun gave their name to a class of peoples who later ruled at Senaar, on the Blue Nile, and who were in some sense a remnant of the former Ethiopian Kingdoms of Napata and Meroe on the Nile, and of the later Axum, the Sanbaritae (Sembritae) of Herodotus in 600 B.C.

These too are the people, or some of them, whom the Arab writers associated with the army of Afrikishu (Afarik) which conquered the West. It would then be very probable, since the Bornu Keyi or so-called Saifawa royal clan claim a connection with Senaar, that the Egyptian Fenh is the same as Fune, the name given to the second Mai of Kanem, and a word which also means both in Kanem and Tebu, the mouth covering (Ar: lithan) of the Tuwareg.

The Arabic word ' lithan ' meaning (1) to kiss, (2) to pound stones (of a camel walking), (3) to muffle, *i.e.*, to cover the mouth, may perhaps have a connection with the Arctic root ' latha '; which means " to exude gum ". It is possible that ' lithan ' were originally ' gum people ' and it was because they were muffled that the word came to mean ' to muffle ', and because a kiss was part of their ritual that the word ' latham ' came to have that meaning, and, further, that the meaning of pounding came because they were 'camel-owners' living in a rocky desert.

In the Southern Sahara and Sudan the words in use for this covering are:—

(1) Fune ... ... Kanuri and Teda.
(2) Amawal ... ... From the Tamashek am—mouth, used by the Fulani and Hausa and Tuwareg themselves.
(3) Atel ... .⎫
(4) Anagud ... ..⎬ by the Tuwareg themselves.
(5) Tesilgemist or Thigel-must ... .⎭

The root of (5) is either sigel or silge, probably sigil, as being analogous to atel and amawel. The Tamashek word for the Talh Acacia (Acacia Seyal) is Asagher. In Kanuri, the Acacia Verek is 'Kindil' while the Acacia Seyal is called 'Kingar', 'Karunga' or 'Karamga', and in Teda "Tahi" is the word.

It is said that a Tuwareg is afraid of the smell of any 'acacia' and if he is near any redolent species of that tree he will closely cover his mouth and nose with the 'lithan'.

This is borne out by the Kanuri words for acacia 'kin-dil' and 'kin-gar', the former of which is a variant for the Kanuri name for the Tuwareg 'Kindin', while the latter contains the same syllable 'kin' (*i.e.*, the Keyi or Kayi), and is the same as the Kanuri name for the 'sun'—Kingar.

The Semitic root 'átr', perfume, aromatic, etc., may perhaps be connected with the Tuwareg 'tara' to burn, and the Aryan 'athravan', while the root 'if', 'af', in 'afa',—pardon, and 'ifn'—smell, seem to be connected with the same category of thought.

Returning then to the Carthaginian Tanit called pene Baal 'the face of Baal', she may perhaps be regarded as the 'ankh' or life (Isis) symbolised by a cross (crossed-twigs) with the orb of the sun above them. That symbol the Egyptian ankh cross would then be the Tamashek 'tifinagh' or 'sign' of the Baal or 'spirit', which causes the manifestation which is the Nana or Ish-tar from which things are borne.

As among the Ethiopians there were 'cattle of the sun' which we may perhaps regard as the cattle of Nana or Ish-tar, so apparently was the Fulani 'cow' originally the 'inn-ek' (Tamashek—child), or nagge (Fulfulde—cow) of Inna = Nana the Great Mother Ishtar or 'the sun'.

It is suggested therefore that the Tuwareg 'veil' was originally a covering worn to protect the Tarkiyi, *i.e.*, (Barbar of a Dir or Barbar encampment) from the sanctity of the Acacia, which was his 'pene Baal'. *i.e.*, manifestation of Baal, so that the sacred aroma should not directly penetrate his nose and mouth.

From the fact that the acacia was a manifestation of El (God), plus 'ite' = 'fire', may have come the female of El, El-Lat, and from 'Lat' came perhaps 'Lath', *i.e.*, what the acacia did, *i.e.*, exude gum or resin, and 'lithan' the protection of the gatherer from the sanctity of the gum.

From the manifestation of the Baal which was 'Puni' or 'Pene', it is suggested that the gum country itself was called Punt, its people Puni or Funi, and the so-called Benu bird was called *Phoinix* 'Fen-ek', all these ideas being connected with the Semitic 'fi', 'fa', or 'fam' = mouth and "ifn" "smell".

	Hausa.	Tamashek.	Kanuri.	Tebu.	Fulfulde.
Sun	Rana	Tafok	Kingal	Ze (Zi)	Nange
Light	Haske	Tafaut	Farak	Washi	N'jairi. Hubbaga
Heat of day	Zafin rana	Tara hôd	Kingal jô	Izzê	Genawi
Morning	Sâfi	Tifaut	Fajar	Bitayı	Weti, Farardu
Moon	Wata	Ayor	Kintagu	Ori	Leuru (yero)
Full moon	Chikkaken wata	Ahador	Kumbal	,,	,, ,,
Moonlight	Farin wata	Timillen Ayor	Nur Kumbalbe	,,	Lelewal
Star	Tamraro	Atar	Silogo	Teski	Hodere
Stars	Tamrari	Itaren	Chilowa	Teskê	Hode
Fire	Wuta	Efeu	Kannu	Wuni	Ite or Yite
Flame	Haske	Tahist	Nur Kannube	Nur wuni	Ite gedon hubba
Smoke	Hayaki	Ahu	Kanje	Izzì (Izzí=shoes)	Churde
Sky	Samma	Ashinna	Kiri	N'guli	Dô; Kamu
Daybreak	Gari ya wayi	Ashel	Dunya Wazinna	Bi Tayyi	Wetgo; Ba abal; Gelle m'bali jam
North	Arewa	Afelle	Yeri; Yalan	Yela	Rewo: woyla: sobire
South	Gusum; kudu	Agus	Anum	Anum	Wargo: fumbina
East	Gabas	Ammana	Gidin	Mâ	Funange
West	Yamma	Ataram	Fute	Ji	Gorgal: hir-nange mutirle:

NOTE ON YAM.
(Girgam No. 18).

The greater portion of the non-Arab tribes which stretch from the Gongola Valley to the Shari, and from the Benue to the Tibesti highlands and Wadai, believe that they originally came from a country called Yam or Yayambal, somewhere to the East of Lake Chad. The idea may be due, in part, to the Muslim influence of Yaman, but its ubiquity and universality seems to point further back than the Muslim era for its origin, and to indicate some language which has long disappeared but was spoken somewhere in the eastern parts of the Sudan or Nile Valley, and possibly beyond.

Closely connected with Yam in the minds of the populations of the Chad basin, who in chief and in particular ascribe their origin to Yam, is the place name spelt Yen, or Yo, or Yau.

There have been many Yos among the Kanuri. There is now Yo on the Komadugu, Yo near Lake Fittri, and another Yo to the South of the Tibesti range. We have also the form Biyo, by which name the peoples of the Baghermi region called the Kanuri. Biu is also a common place name, the first Biyo or Wayo being situated near Dagana in Kanem.

A characteristic of all the 'Yos' seems to be that they were near water. In the Hausa language iyo means to 'swim', miyo means 'water' (spittle), and the ordinary word for water is r-iyo-a (ruwa). In the Kanuri language on the other hand, the word for water is Nk'i or N'gi. In Tamashek, a river is egireu, and a rivulet Anghi (Kanuri N'ki). In Songhay we have the word 'hi' or 'di' = water, and in Tebu 'Yi' is water. In Fulfulde water is n'diam, and blood is yi-am.

There seems then no doubt that among the earlier or "Gara" Hamite tribes, the simple vowel sound 'i' denoted 'water', particularly moving water, and was pronounced variously as 'yi' or 'ye'—the one sound shading off into the other.

In Hausa the idea of 'movement in water' seems to have caused the derived sense 'to do' in 'yi'.* It would seem further that since this sound denoting water is found in compounds, especially in the case of the suffixing languages of the Eastern Sudan like Kanuri and Teda, that they are a good deal older than the languages of the type of Tamashek and Hausa, for in the former the sound meaning water was apparently compounded at an early period with the commonest suffixes such as 'an' (anna), or 'am' (amma), signifying 'peoples', 'ri' the locative suffix, 'bi' or 'be' (genitival) 'wa' (possessive suffix), and 'di' (place or land of).

Thus Ye-di 'land of Ye' was the land area in Lake Chad, whence the inhabitants of the islands were called Yedi or Yidina (Budduma). Ye-bur-di 'land of the Yebu' or Yebur, originally meant the 'water people' or people near or beyond water—to the

---

* cf. the expression ya yio dari = 'night came on', just as 'water' might flood a plain.

Kanuri or Tebu, then their ancestral enemies (Yebur), the Tuwareg.

Yam-di-Kowwa,—in old songs means the rocky land of Yam (Borku).

Ye-ri or *Ye-lan* = the north, literally ' water place ' in Kanuri.

Ye-an (Yen)—' Borku ' is the region of the Jurab (Lake) also (*vide* above) called Ye-am (Yam).

Ye-uyo or *Yau*—' riverain '.

Yau-ri (Yauri)—' Place on the river '.

In Hausa Yau (Yo) = ' to-day '. Yini = ' a day ' (as opposed to night). In Songhay the ' Hi-koy ' was ' King of the water '. In Bornu also a variant of Yedi (Budduma) is Hedi. Similarly the title Yeri-ma (chief of the north ' Yeri ') had a variant in the title Hiri-ma or Iyrima, who was, however, the chief who had control of the East. The ordinary word for east in use, however, is gi-di or gi-din, which seems to denote the land (di) of the Kiyi or Kayi, *i.e.*, Tuwareg, originally invaders from the East, who lived in Makida (Kordofan).

It seems therefore probable that the Kanuri language was originally spoken by people who—

(a) were bounded on the South by people like themselves (anna);

(b) were bounded on the East by Tuwareg Kayi (Kindin);

(c) were bounded on the North by either a river or the sea.

Such a region in Africa is provided by either the horn of Africa (Somaliland) or by the regions contained in the bend of the Nile, South of Wadi Halfa, assuming that the period were remote enough.

Which of these two it may have been, seems to be suggested by the fact that the ancient Egyptians called the region of Philae (Pilak) and Aswan (Syene) Ye, and that Yam was the name by which they knew the country to the South of it, West of the Nile. No doubt the Egyptians called places as we do by the name by which they were known to the inhabitants.

The fact that in addition to " water " being in Kanuri N'gi (the root of N'gi-ri, N'gir, whence " Niger ", in Tebu " yi " and in Songhay " hi ", it is, in Tamashek, angi or egiriu and in Hausa ri(wa), does not probably mean more than that the two latter tongues took over a pre-existing word for ' water ', as might be shown to have been the case in many other instances. The Kanuri and Songhay group of languages are probably much older in North Central Africa than Tamashek and Hausa, but the fact that in Hausa this " Gara " word for ' water ' is used to express the diurnal round of the sun (rana) is interesting because it seems to show that its use was derived from the cosmographic ideas current in Egypt about the sun-boat's daily course, *i.e.*, the Hausa ' yini ' ' day ' was perhaps originally the water on which the sun boat floated to the West. The place name Yam having come to have significance as the home of the " Gara " from whom they derived their culture was therefore applied by the Hausas or pre-Hausas to the place of departed spirits—Yamma or the " West ".

It is noticeable that whereas in Arabic the word Yaman

(South) means also the right hand ', the Tamashek agus (South) becomes in Hausa the word hagu (left hand), while the Hausa equivalent for the Tamashek agus—gussum—has a variant ' kudu ', perhaps the Arabic kudus ' sacred '.

In Kanuri it will be observed the only name among those for the cardinal points, which refers to the sun is ' Fute ' the West—derived from the same root (fu—to blaze or burn) as the Hausa fudo ', used of the sun ' to rise '.

The differentiation in the meaning of Yam between Kanuri and Hausa, means, it is suggested, that whereas the original Ye-am (people of Ye = Elephantine) originally " North ", was the place of departed spirits and belonged to the nomenclature of the Nobatac or Tebu races who lived in Yam West of the Nile, the name was adopted with a similar connotation by Blemmyes or Tuwareg tribes living East of the Nile who adopted Egyptian cosmic ideas which they transmitted to Tamashek and Hausa.

Among the Hausa and Tuwareg ' Yam ' ' West ' is the ' Kibla ', and hence " agus " is South and ' hagu ' in Hausa means the left hand.

Among the Kanuri on the contrary, Yam is North-west and is the ' Kibla ' and home of the race, while its root, *i.e.*, yi or ye ' water ' (of the Nile) remains their term for North, *i.e.*, Ye-lan, or Yeri.

In Kanuri, Yer-wa (Yerwa), Hausa Yelwa means " riches ", " prosperity ".

It is suggested that this word is in substance identical with ' Meroe ' or ' Beruat ' the capital of the Ethiopian Kingdom, the wealth of which the desert Kash (Tebu) no doubt envied.

That the tongue of the Kash or one of their tongues has survived as the modern Brabra is natural enough, as natural as that the inscriptions at Meroe, are due to conquering races, and are not in the tongue of the Kash, who later were called Brabra on the Nile, and Tebu further West.

According to M. Desplagnes,* throughout the Nigerian Sudan and Sahara, conquered Hamite races were called " Gara " and were " red men ", shepherds, who introduced cattle, goats and sheep. He also holds that the Gara introduced iron-working (agreeing presumably with Marmol's statement that ' iron-working ' was introduced into the Sahara by the Gaetuli) and that everywhere they formed the colonies of herdsmen and traders whom are met with under the names of Sonnike, Sarakwolli, Wakore, Wangara, etc.

" Relics of their passage through the Sahara are found in " Adrar and elsewhere, where ruins occur, said by the Moors and " Barbars to have been made by the Gagara who occupied the " country before them."

Though we may not follow M. Desplagnes in all his speculations, thus much seems true, and to account for the factor which is common to the Fulbe, Tebu, Kanuri and Songhay, and to some extent to their languages.

* La Plateau Central Nigerian. Pari Emile Larose 1907.

That factor moreover can only be the races who by the Egyptians were called the " vile Kash " who were later dominated and made " servile " by the " veiled Tuwareg ".

In the Kanuri language " -am " and " -wa " are both suffixes meaning people. The singular of both is formed by prefixing " k ".

Kam, meaning (1) man; (2) person.

Kwa, meaning man; warrior.

A variant and older form of " -am " is " -an "—the form used mainly by the Tebu and by the ancient Egyptians to denote these desert peoples.

It is noticeable that among the Kanuri, particularly the Kanembu and Bulala part of them, the proper word for " The King's Sceptre " or " Mace " (commonly called the Bâbu), is " Ka ", and this appears to be the same as the Egyptian syllabic hieroglyph $\times$ = " mace ".

One is tempted therefore to conjecture that this early word for " mace "—" ka ", and the Kanuri word for Barbars Kayi or Kiyi are connected, and that Kayin or Kin was originally a form paralled to Kam and Kwa being composed of k(a), the mace, *i.e.*, " ruler " " King ", and " an ", " n ", the people.

The two forms Kinin (Darfur) and Kindin (Bornu) would thus only differ in this that the latter contains the Kanuri " di " = land, and is really k-an-di- in " mace people "—" land people " = Kindin.

If this is correct a parity of reasoning would make the title Gâna, the ruler of Gana or Gunata in the West, similarly the " mace " (Ga or Ka since K and G are interchangeable) of the " an " or anna people, *i.e.*, Gara. In like manner the owners of the " maces ", *i.e.*, the ruling race, were in both cases not the earlier Kushite Gara (Garamantes), etc., but Ibn Khaldun's second race of Sanhaja (San-gara), *i.e.*, the Tuwareg races, the Kindin of the Kanuri.

The chiefs of these same ruling Barbars were called by the Hausas Sara-ki, and by the Songhays Ki-sara, while the Zaghawa (Wadai) word for father is Kisar, Sara and Sek being apparently the softened Sudanese equivalent of the Barbar sagh = a camp.

This word sagh (-sek or sar (sara) in the Sudan) apparently belonged to the Gara languages, the pre-Tuwareg languages, being a " camp " as opposed to a " garu " or town.

In the West generally speaking, -sagh is prefixed to the tribal name, as *e.g.*, in Sek-mara (camp of the Mara or Mellians) Sara-Kollê (San-Kore or Wa-Kore) Sara-Dina, Sara-Yamo, Sag-Gazar, (Cheggazar) Sag-Gutu (Sokoto), Sag-Tala (Siktala), while in the Chad region and the East, it is usually a suffix as *e.g.*, in Dama-sak, Ama-sak (Amsaka), Gama-sek, Ma-sek (Musgu), Wu-shek, etc.

The Tuwareg races apparently adopted the term; hence in Tamashek a camp, originally a camp of the Ama (Gara races), is Ama-(s)zagh (Amasagh); though (this group of languages using prefixes) when they used Sek (Zagh) as a descriptive epithet of a place or people, they placed it in front of the defining term for the people, *e.g.*, Zaghawa (dwellers in camps) a **Tuwareg** tribal name, Sig-Gidin(m) the oasis North of Kauwar where Gidin (Kindin) settled, Sak-kala (camp of the N'gala or Kala, *i.e.*, Gara), Sag-wa (camp of the Zaghawa *vide* Idrisi).

The genesis of the Tuwareg in the Central and Western Sahara seems clear not only from Ibn Khaldun's works supported by Ibn Battuta El Bekri and Idrisi but from modern traditions and the chronicle of Ahir which reads:—

"The origin of the Sultanate of Ahir is that four tribes, "the Iteseyen, Jedâlanan, Azaranan, and Afadanan, came to "Ahir from Aujila (Fezzan) and drove out the Sudanese from "Ahir and dwelt there a long time without a Sultan."

Later, so it is recorded, five tribes of the San-Dala, which in common are called Imakitan, made a Sultan of Ahir A.H. 807, A.D. 1404.

The Fulani of Adamawa call the races of Bornu in general (*i.e.*, the Teda-Kanuri) Koleyen, which is equivalent to the terms Wa-Kore, Sara-Kolle, Kolon, Kola, Gola, etc., terms which are similarly used by them to denote the early Saharan races North and West of the Upper Niger in contrast to the Torudu (Toronke) or inhabitants of Futa Toro), which formed the mother stock of the Fulbe themselves.

It can hardly be doubted that these races are substantially the same as the "Ahel Gara" mentioned in the Diwan, *i.e.*, the pre-Tuwareg Garawan or Garamantes.

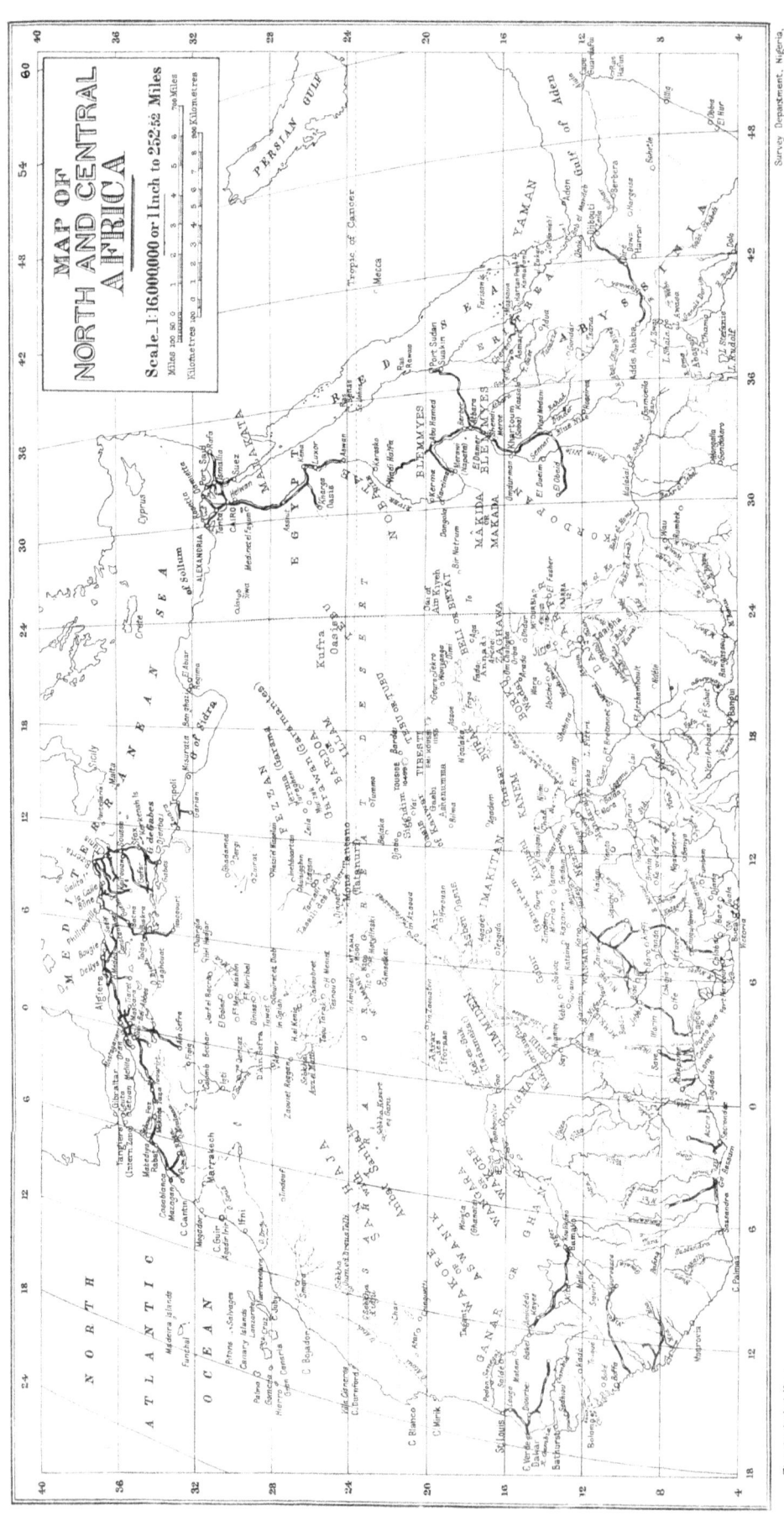

For Product Safety Concerns and Information please contact our EU
representative GPSR@taylorandfrancis.com
Taylor & Francis Verlag GmbH, Kaufingerstraße 24, 80331 München, Germany

www.ingramcontent.com/pod-product-compliance
Lightning Source LLC
Chambersburg PA
CBHW081830300426
44116CB00014B/2538